Cooking Through History

A Comprehensive Manual
on How to Give A Theme Party

*With Instructions for Ten Dinner Parties, a Cocktail Party,
a Ladies' Lunch, and a Family Brunch*

Cooked up by Claire S. Cabot,
with the help of family and friends

To My friend with
THE killer serve!
Best wishes
Claire

Image credits appear on page 156.
Cover photograph by Ben Galante.

Book and cover design by J. Putnam Design, www.jputnamdesign.com

ISBN 13: 978-1-533307-84-2
ISBN 10: 1-533-30784-9

DEDICATION

This book is dedicated to my wonderful husband, Sam, who lovingly donned wigs, period costumes, and his great sense of humor for the parties discussed in this book. He also did all the research for the appropriate alcoholic beverages and music for each theme party.

The second dedication is to my daughter, Wickes Anne Helmboldt, who has been giving me good advice about my writing since she was in pigtails.

The third dedication is to our wonderful friends who participated in researching each of the candidates we chose for our theme parties. Sam and I learned more delicious facts from our guests than we ever could have acquired on our own.

I would be remiss if I did not mention the wonderful staff in the Rare Books Division of the Boston Public Library, who supplied me with original samples of the handwriting of each of the stellar individuals for our parties. Viewing these samples gave such enormous insight into the various characters.

Contents

This book is for people who love the long, slow, artful discourse of conversation against a backdrop of delicious food. My wonderful husband Sam and I love commensality (the act of eating together) and consider a dinner party a success when guests leave after midnight! *Cooking Through History* has given us another excuse to collect friends. It is an exploration and celebration of individuals who strove to make a difference in the world. For each party, we chose to focus on a writer, musician, or statesperson with a birthday in the month when the party took place. Many of the picks were prompted by our travels.

Cooking Through History describes how you can host interactive events for your guests to heighten their intellectual curiosity. We live in a busy time, in a world that seems increasingly chaotic. These special occasions afford an opportunity to learn more about famous figures and to enter into their worlds for a time. This book describes the themes we chose, but the real purpose of this humble offering is larger: it is to invite you to use *Cooking Through History* as a primer for your own gatherings.

As always, I had a wonderful time putting this book together. Writing cookbooks, for me, has been a journey and an evolution. For this book, each party offered an opportunity to think of something innovative for the next event. I have met wonderful people along the way who helped me find unusual ingredients or gave me tips on how to cook something. Our local butcher believes that, because ovens vary, the only way to test for doneness is with a meat thermometer. Always try to develop a dialogue with people who sell you food and compliment them on steering you in the right direction.

A good friend suggested I write "postmortems" of each party, which I thought was an excellent idea. Trading intelligence with my dear husband or another guest after the festivities is often as much fun as the actual party. Meals carry memories—good, bad, and ugly. Not all dinners turn out to be joyful, but a heated discussion over politics or a family drama can make a chocolate soufflé even sweeter. A Christmas dinner when your favorite dog ate the roast or the cat licked the soup on a well-set table lends itself to a mutual bonding over "remember when."

My mother gave my sister and me the legacy of good cooking. From the beginning of my life, sitting at the dining-room table having a good meal was a major part of our family culture. We lived in Manchester, Massachusetts, and every summer my mother's loquacious relatives would escape the heat of Maryland and visit us on the North Shore of Boston. My sister and I always knew this meant at least one lobster dinner! These evenings were happy times. I quickly learned all the stories, many of which were repeated each year. I would like to think that this tradition of commensality has been passed along to all of our children and grandchildren.

The therapeutic healing of cooking a meal for family and friends has always been an outlet for me, during good times and bad. My dear father died at the age of ninety-five, around two o'clock in the afternoon. He sent my stepmother a dozen roses for their anniversary, had lunch, and slipped away. My cousin Chester laughed and said, "Isn't that typical? No one in our family ever likes to miss a meal!"

My beloved second husband, Sam, loves giving parties as much as I do. I could not have written this book without him. He is a good master planner, often keeping flowcharts of the guest list, helping design the invitations, and diligently checking off the acceptances. He has been the sommelier even though we both decided we did not have the expertise to give advice regarding the wines. Sam also was the researcher for the musical accompaniment for each dinner. He has been a wonderful sport, donning wigs and period costumes when the appropriate occasion arrived.

I would be the first to admit that not all of our efforts were successful. Here are a few points to remember: A. Do not attempt a theme party for a group of friends who have not seen each other for a long time. Understandably, they will be more interested in focusing on each other than on the chosen character. B. This is first and foremost a cookbook. Some fascinating characters did not inspire an interesting menu and were rejected for that reason—General MacArthur comes instantly to mind. C. Not all of my dishes were successful. Some guests had much better suggestions, which they shared. This book is designed as a learning tool for everyone, so encourage your guests to help out. D. Be kind to your guests who call and decide they just aren't suited for this type of evening.

The genesis of *Cooking Through History* began when we were in Egypt, motoring down the Nile. We were on a trip organized by Dartmouth University, with many of Sam's retired classmates from the Psi Upsilon fraternity. I had just finished my first cookbook, *A Short History of Ingre-*

dients, and was trying to think of a topic for my next book. One of the wives, whom I had not met before the trip, lived in Colorado and wrote a small cooking column in her husband's newspaper. From her experience, she felt people often wanted to have full menus planned for them.

This thought percolated in my brain for the next couple of months. We then had a wonderful invitation from some friends to visit them at their country house, Whitmuir, in the Selkirk area of Scotland. The purpose of the visit was going to be a series of driven shoots. Sam, an avid hunter, was thrilled. We went in January.

For some, the prospect of winter weather in Scotland would be daunting. However, for two old, tough New Englanders, the climate of Scotland—even when it snows—does not seem to bring the bitter, chilly cold of our winters. I find the open, rolling hills of the border areas of Scotland breathtakingly beautiful at any time of year. We go from one beautiful estate to another in quest of pheasants. It is not uncommon to be standing in a pasture with sheep or cows, in front of a plantation of pines, waiting for the beaters to drive out the birds. The farm animals are remarkably unperturbed by the shooters. These hunts are accompanied by generous food breaks about every two hours. The first break is about eleven o'clock in the morning. The fare often consists of sloe gin, hot soup, small sausages, or meat pastries. This is followed by more hunting until about twelve thirty, when we go to a lovely house or barn for a substantial lunch, often consisting of shepherd's pie. After several more hours in the field, tea is served with small sandwiches and often a large, delicious cake.

There was a lot of discussion around the dinner table at Whitmuir about the upcoming Robert Burns evening, which takes place in all sectors of society throughout Scotland. It is traditionally held on January 25, his birthday. The Scots often refer to him lovingly as Bobby Burns. Specific dishes are served, certain poems are read, and toasts are given.

When our driver picked us up at Whitmuir and drove us to Edinburgh, I found myself conducting another detailed interview regarding the menu and procedures of the Robert Burns evening that he and his friends have at their local club.

Now comes a true confession: one of my favorite jobs was being a feature writer for a magazine called *The Resident* in southeastern Connecticut. The periodical prided itself on being a good-news publication; we highlighted interesting people, historic locations, and events in our community. I always walked away from interviews having enormous respect for my subjects. I noticed that they all had a passion for life and dedication to their given disciplines.

I came away from Scotland with an idea. Sam and I would host a Robert Burns evening in Beverly Farms, Massachusetts, and see how the evening went. *Cooking Through History* was taking shape. If the dinner party was a success, we would continue.

Analyzing people's handwriting is one of my guilty pleasures, so occasionally in this book I have included a handwriting analysis of the given personality. My sincerest thanks go to the Rare Books Division of the Boston Public Library, whose staff generously allowed me to see original copies of documents.

Getting Started

In many ways, giving a dinner party is not unlike performing a three-act play. You have the invitation, the table setting, and the grand finale of the meal with music or entertainment. I like to plan ahead. Murphy's Law usually rears its ugly head, and inevitably some unforeseen problem arises on the day of the party. The more you have things under control, the more relaxed you will be.

The Invitation

Many people send their invitations online these days. But not being a very sophisticated computer-savvy person, I usually send them by snail mail. I try to make each invitation reflect the period and personality of the character being highlighted. Let your imagination go wild, and be as creative as possible. An exciting invitation bodes well for an exciting party.

Table Settings

Table settings are fun. They can be elaborate or simple. When I first went back to work after having my children, I would often get a call from my first husband saying he wanted to bring someone home for dinner. I'd call home and get my children to set the table. Their fresh eyes and enthusiasm for decorating place cards and choosing a variety of colored table mats (not always matching) was refreshing. They had great fun helping out. This is a long way of saying that anything goes. If you get tired of what is in your closet, go to some secondhand stores or tag sales. You will be amazed at what you can find. I try to create table settings that reflect the character and era of the celebrity we are highlighting.

Music

We try to pick music reflective of the time and spirit of the evening. There is a lot of latitude in this category. The Internet is most helpful in conducting research.

Menu

I love to read cookbooks and give a lot of thought to the menu. For me, it is part of the fun. Sam says I agonize about it, but I tell him it is like him trying to decide what fly he is going to pack for our annual fishing trip on the Rio Petrohué in Ensenada, Chile.

CHAPTER 1

January Dinner to Celebrate

Robert Burns, Scottish Poet

"Dare to be honest and fear no labor."
- Robert Burns (January 25, 1759-July 21, 1796)

Robert Burns was born in a two-room cottage in Alloway, Ayrshire, Scotland. The son of a tenant farmer, Robert was the first of seven children. His father was an avid reader and insisted that all of his children learn this valuable skill. Robert had little formal education, but once he learned to read, he educated himself by reading the English writers. His father died when Robert was fifteen, which, sadly, propelled him into manhood.

Along with his brother Gilbert, Robert bought a small farm in Mossgiel. He began writing poetry in his spare time and often took inspiration from his surroundings. One of his early poems was about a mouse, and many of his love poems were dedicated to a pretty lady named Jean Armour. The farm failed, but by 1786 Robert had published his first book of poetry in his native Scottish dialect. His love affair with Jean was not successful and he hoped to earn enough money from the sale of his poetry to escape to Jamaica. However, when the book was a success, he decided to take the earnings and move to Edinburgh.

Eventually, love won out. Robert returned to Ellisland, near Dumfries, with money in his pocket, and married Jean Armour. After another failed farm, Burns moved his family to Dumfries and became an excise man, inspecting products and collecting taxes for the government. This nonlaboring clerk's job was more in line with his poetry career.

Burns is noted for being one of the founders of modern romantic poetry, which celebrates the simple pleasures of life and the human heart. Many literary historians feel he was as much an originator of romanticism as were Blake and Chaucer. Burns's talent for writing verse quickly became legendary. Burns is reported to have written his famous and very lengthy "Tam O'Shanter" in one sitting. Today we read his poetry in English, but much was made of the rhythm of Burns's verses, which were written in his native dialect. By 1791, Burns began writing lyrics to many old Scottish tunes; "Auld Lang Syne" comes instantly to mind.

Robert Burns also had a wild side. Pictures of him show a good-looking young man who is purported to have loved pretty women, drink, and general carousing. Would we have expected anything else from one of our favorite poets? Sadly, his lifestyle caught up with him, and he died at age thirty-four. Luckily, the royalties from his writings supported his wife and four children. Robert Burns touched many people's lives with his works. Indeed, there are some forty statues of him around the world.

The first Robert Burns night was held on the anniversary of his death on July 21, 1796, in Alloway, Scotland. In 1801, a Burns club was formed in Ayrshire by many of the men who had known him. They changed the celebration of the Burns dinners to his birthdate, January 25.

Handwriting of Robert Burns

While doing some research for another book, I visited the Rare Books Division of the Boston Public Library. Massachusetts residents are lucky to have such a marvelous facility so accessible to the public. When you finally get through the layers of security to the top floor, you find the friendly and knowledgeable staff. For fun, and because I do handwriting analysis, I decided to inspect Robert Burns's handwriting. It is difficult to describe what a thrill it is for me to see another person's handwriting, especially one who lived in the 1700s. Burns's personality instantly came to life.

His handwriting shows an outgoing person who enjoyed the company of others. He was empathetic and probably a good listener. He loved a good argument or a worthy discussion, where he could use his quick wit and knowledge of words to make his point. It comes as no surprise that Burns scores well in the realm of imagination, though he wrote about things within the context of his daily life and themes of everyday people. Burns was not disposed to exploration of a philosophical nature. He was a good decision maker, did not deliberate, and had excellent executive capabilities.

Claire and Sam Cabot ask you to
please join us for
a celebration of the life of
Robert Burns
(January 25, 1759–July 21, 1796)

[date, time, and location]

Please bring a poem or fact to share.
Wearing plaid is appreciated but not required.
RSVP [telephone number and e-mail address]

Table Setting

January is a cold month, and one has the desire to cover up with extra clothing. This sentiment translated onto our dining-room table. This book may be as much about true confessions as it is about cooking: one of my guilty pleasures in life is table linens. I wanted something heavy and ended up using an old brocade tablecloth that had belonged to my mother. It is a soft moss green. I paired the tablecloth with some off-white brocade napkins. If you don't have a tablecloth, you can be happy with table mats. In many pubs around Scotland, they celebrate Burns's birthday with cutlery on the bare table.

Imagining the lighting in the 1700s was easy. Without electricity, the room would have had low light. In various cupboards, I found a collection of candlesticks and placed them strategically around the dining room. Colored candles can be fun, but not for this evening. Ivory seemed to work well without making a statement and picked up the color of the napkins.

Clearly, it was too cold to use flowers from our garden, and fresh greens would have seemed too much like Christmas, which had just passed. There is a large vegetable dish that goes with my china, which I rarely use to serve food, so I put that in the center of the table. Now, for the checklist: salt and pepper, butter plates on the upper left corner, water glasses and wine glasses on the right. Candy dishes at each end.

Scotland is famous for their Scotch. Sam suggested we serve malt whiskey in small glasses set at everyone's place. If you don't have ten small uniform glasses, try to create a motif with alternating ones. Most of our friends like to drink wine, but beer would also be appropriate.

Music

Scotland is famous for bagpipes, which were introduced in the fifteenth century by the Gaels from Ireland. Certain clans were considered "piping clans," the Highlands being the most prominent. My research showed that bagpipe music is played traditionally when the haggis, a type of pudding popular in Scotland, is brought to the table. The Internet is a huge resource, and I was able to find some bagpipe music on a CD. We also listened to the folk music of a 1960s group called the Corries as well as that of Ian Campbell, another pleasing performer. Once again, you can find his and the Corries' CDs on the Internet. The Corries' rendition of "The Wild Mountain Thyme" is guaranteed to put everyone in a joyful spirit. It is difficult to hear a lot of the Corries' music without wanting to join in the singing, even if you are not familiar with the lyrics.

Robert Burns spent many long hours putting words to traditional Scottish ballads. In 1788, he wrote "Auld Lang Syne," which idiomatically can be translated as "long, long ago." The song is sung at the end of the year and also at funerals and the close of the Boy Scout Jamboree. The phrase "We'll take a cup of kindness yet, for auld lang syne" positively reduces me to tears.

The traditional grace said before dinner is Burns's "Selkirk Grace":

> Some hae meat and canna eat,
> And some wad eat that want it;
> But we hae meat, and we can eat,
> And sae let the Lord be thankit.

Menu for Ten

Hors d'oeuvres
Smoked Scottish Salmon on Pumpernickel Bread with Dill

Soup Course
Cock-a-Leekie Soup with Chopped Parsley

Main Course
Haggis
Roast Leg of Lamb with Mint Jelly
Roasted Turnips, Carrots, Potatoes, and Onions

Cheese Course
Stilton and Brie Cheeses with Grapes and Crackers

Dessert
Sticky Toffee Pudding with Sauce
Single-Malt Scotch Fudge

Recipes

Smoked Salmon on Pumpernickel Bread
Preparation time: 15 minutes

10 small pieces dark pumpernickel bread
3 tablespoons butter, at room temperature
8 ounces smoked salmon
1 bunch dill

Remove the crusts from the bread and spread with butter. Put a slice of salmon on each piece of bread, and cut the bread in half. Decorate with dill.

Chef's Note: You can make these canapés up in the morning and wrap them carefully. Refrigerate and then bring them to room temperature before serving. Usually I like having two hors d'oeuvres for a dinner party. But since this is such a heavy meal, I decided to serve just one. If you feel you need another predinner nibble, you can always serve a few bowls of nuts.

Cock-a-Leekie Soup
Preparation time: 45 minutes

3 cups chopped leeks
3 tablespoons butter
8 cups good chicken stock (see Chef's Note)
3 cups diced cooked skinless chicken
4 cups chopped prunes
¾ cup chopped parsley

Wash the leeks thoroughly in cold water. Open up the leaves to make sure all the sand is removed. Chop up into smallish pieces, leaving a little water on them from their bath. Melt the butter in a large pot on top of the stove. Add the leeks, cover, and sauté them over low heat for fifteen minutes or until tender. Stir often so they don't stick to the bottom of the pan. Add the chicken stock, cover, and simmer for another twenty-five minutes. Finally, add the diced chicken and prunes. Simmer on low, uncovered, for ten more minutes. Serve in shallow bowls, and decorate with fresh parsley.

Chef's Note: Definitely make this soup a day or two before your party. The quality of your chicken stock is going to determine the quality of this over-the-top, superflavorful, get-to-the-core-of-your-soul soup.

Haggis
Preparation time: 25 minutes

Finding haggis was not easy. I spoke to several butchers, without any luck. Always, but always, develop a relationship with the wonderful people behind the counter who provide you with food. You can learn from their expertise. After many phone calls, I found a young woman who had a specialty shop devoted to products from Scotland. She carried both canned and frozen haggis. The frozen is better, but the canned is passable.

Don't be surprised if the majority of people you speak with don't know what haggis is, let alone eat it. It is the inside of a sheep's stomach mixed with oatmeal and spices. You probably will find it more appealing if you just think of haggis as the Scottish national dish.

½ cup butter
3 pounds haggis

Add butter to an electric frying pan. If you don't have one, cook on top of the stove. When the butter has melted, add the haggis and cook over medium to low heat for around thirty minutes. To me, the haggis looks like scrapple. Cover and keep warm on low heat until ready to serve. Place a small amount on each plate.

Chef's Note: In our case, we wanted to give each person a small bit of haggis to taste. If you think your guests would like larger portions, double the recipe.

Roast Leg of Lamb
Preparation time: 15 minutes

1 (3½- to 4-pound) leg of lamb, bone in

Salt and pepper
1 bunch fresh rosemary

Preheat oven to 350 degrees. Wash the lamb and dry with paper towels. Remove the heavy fat from the outside, and cover with salt, pepper, and rosemary. Place in a roasting pan on a rack, with a little water in the bottom of the pan. For medium rare, cook twenty minutes per pound to an internal temperature of 145 degrees; for medium well done, twenty-five minutes per pound to an internal temperature of 160 degrees; and for well done, thirty minutes per pound to an internal temperature of 170 degrees.

Chef's Note: When you remove the roast from the oven, cover it with aluminum foil for twenty minutes to let the juices recede, and then slice thinly.

Roasted Turnips, Carrots, Potatoes, and Onions
Preparation time: 30 minutes

5 pounds turnips
5 pounds potatoes
3 pounds carrots
3 pounds onions
¼ cup vegetable or olive oil
1 tablespoon each of oregano, basil, and parsley
Salt and pepper

Preheat oven to 350 degrees. Scrub the vegetables. Cut the bottoms and tops off the turnips, and peel them along with the potatoes and carrots. Cut the vegetables into easy-to-eat sizes. Remove the outer skin of the onions and cut in quarters. Place all the vegetables in a large casserole dish, and coat with the oil. Toss to coat each piece. Then add the oregano, basil, and parsley, with generous amounts of salt and pepper. Cover and bake for one hour, or until the vegetables are tender.

Chef's Note: Vegetables can be cooked the day before and reheated for twenty-five minutes in a 350-degree oven. Make sure the dish is at room temperature before reheating.

Stilton and Brie Cheese with Grapes and Crackers
Preparation time: 15 minutes

1 large bunch seedless grapes
3 pounds Stilton cheese
2 pounds Brie cheese
1 box Carr's water crackers

Arrange the cheese and grapes on a long platter. Pass the crackers in a basket.

Chef's Note: Bring the cheese to room temperature for at least three hours before serving your guests. You cannot believe what a difference this makes in the flavor.

Sticky Toffee Pudding
Preparation time: 25 minutes

3 cups pitted dates
2 teaspoons baking soda
3 cups sifted all-purpose flour
1 teaspoon salt
2 teaspoons baking powder
1 cup unsalted butter, at room temperature
1½ cups sugar
2 teaspoons vanilla extract
4 eggs

Preheat the oven to 350 degrees. Grease and flour a Bundt pan. Boil two cups of water in a deep pot. Add the dates and stir. After the mixture has returned to a boil, add the baking soda. The mixture will foam; remove immediately from the heat and cover. Allow to cool. Add the mixture to a food processor and pulse quickly. Do not overblend.

Sift the flour, salt, and baking powder in a small bowl, and set aside. Using an electric mixer, beat the butter, sugar, and vanilla until smooth. Beat in the eggs one at a time. For the final step, alternate between adding half the date mixture and half the sifted flour mixture. After this is well blended, place into the Bundt mold. Bake for sixty minutes. Test for doneness by inserting a knife in the center. When it comes out clean, the pudding is done. Cool for half an hour before removing the pudding from the pan.

Chef's Note: This cake is delicious just as is, but the sauce gives it added flavor.

Sauce
Preparation time: 15 minutes

2 cups brown sugar
12 tablespoons unsalted butter
¾ cup heavy cream
3 teaspoons brandy

1½ teaspoons vanilla
½ teaspoon salt

Put the brown sugar, butter, and cream into a saucepan, and cook over medium heat until the mixture boils. Whisk thoroughly until the sugar has dissolved. Lower the heat to simmer, add brandy and vanilla, and continue to whisk for another couple of minutes. When ready to serve, cut the cake and cover with a bit of the sauce.

Chef's Note: Some recipes call for smoothing the cake with the toffee sauce, but I like this approach. If you have any leftover cake, wrap it up carefully and freeze it. The sauce also freezes nicely.

Single-Malt Scotch Fudge
Preparation time: 25 minutes

8 ounces unsweetened chocolate
2 tablespoons butter
2 pounds confectioner's sugar
2 eggs
⅓ cup heavy cream
¼ cup single-malt Scotch

Butter an eight-inch-by-eight-inch dish, and set aside. Place the chocolate and butter in a double boiler, and heat very slowly at a low temperature. Do not rush this process. While this mixture melts, sift the sugar to ensure smoothness, and set aside. Beat the eggs, cream, and Scotch until frothy. Gradually add the sugar a little at a time. Beat this mixture until it is smooth. When the chocolate and butter have completely melted, add to the egg mixture. Beat quickly, and then place in the buttered dish. Allow the fudge to cool at room temperature. Place in the refrigerator or a cool pantry for an hour before cutting.

Chef's Note: If the mixture becomes hard too fast, heat the back of a large spoon or spatula under hot water and run the warm instrument over the fudge.

Postmortem
Our first theme party venture was a major triumph, from our standpoint. Clearly, the success of these evenings will rest solely with your most enthusiastic and intellectually curious friends. Our guests that evening were positively plucked from central casting. One brave friend started off by offering to read the blessing in a Scottish dialect. Everyone wore a bit of plaid, whether it was a long evening skirt, trousers sewn of

the Campbell tartan, a tie, or a shawl. The cast looked stunning decked out in their Scottish regalia. One noble guest could trace his ancestry back to Robert Burns. We looked at him with total reverence!

Many people at the table had been to Scotland and waxed blissful over their holidays. It is truly a lovely country. When you are there, it is easy to see how the magnificent rolling hills and tamed pastures became an inspiration for Robert Burns in his writing. As the whiskey took hold and the candles dipped, one gentleman confessed to having a love affair with a lass in Dumfries and Galloway during the summer of his eighteenth year. By this time of the evening, Sam had perfected his Scottish accent.

A really fun part of the evening was learning about Robert Burns from one other. One knowledgeable soul informed us that there is a statue of him, by Henry Kitson, at One Winthrop Square in Boston. The statue was erected in 1920 by the Burns Memorial Association and was originally placed on the Fenway. The next time we went into Boston, Sam and I found the statue we had probably walked past many times without noticing. The statue is truly lovely. Burns is in full stride, accompanied by his dog, Luath, the Gaelic word for "swift." The bronze statue clearly reflects Burns's love of the outdoors. One can easily imagine Burns striding over his beloved farmland.

CHAPTER 2

February Dinner to Celebrate the Life of

Samuel de Champlain, Founder of New France

"I directed the men in our barque to approach near the savages,
and hold their arms in readiness to do their duty in case they notice
any movement of these people against us."
- Samuel de Champlain,
(1574-December 25, 1635)

Samuel de Champlain was born in the southern coastal port city of Brouage, located on the Bay of Biscay in the Aunis province of France, sometime in 1574. Champlain came from a family made up of not only famous mariners, but also cartographers. He became a talented writer and wrote several books about his adventures. If it is true that early memories shape many aspects of our later life, Champlain could not have had a more appropriate upbringing. During the sixteenth century, Brouage was a center for trade. It was said that you could hear as many as twenty different languages when you walked down the street. With these visitors came an opportunity for natives who spoke different languages to make money by serving people from other cultures. Champlain had a curiosity about diverse customs, as well as a lifelong passion for other languages. He was particularly intrigued by Native American languages and probably spoke ten languages by the end of his lifetime.

Champlain's early career began in the French army during the reign of King Henry IV. During this time, he purportedly went on several secret missions. He was hired by his uncle to carry Spanish troops to Cádiz. From there, Champlain sailed with a Spanish captain on his uncle's ship to the West Indies and Mexico. The two-year journey gave Champlain valuable insights into the Spanish approach to colonization. He was impressed with the manner in which the Spaniards outfitted their ships, bringing many vegetables and building materials as well as a priest and a master craftsmen. However, Champlain was appalled at the attitude of the Spanish toward the local inhabitants. The Spanish were highly abusive and showed no respect for local cultures.

Champlain reported this back to King Henry IV in a detailed report. The king was so impressed that he gave Champlain an annual pension and made him an official geographer of the court. One of his duties was to interview fishermen who had gone to North America, from Newfoundland to Nantucket, in search of fertile areas for fishing and trapping furs. Both Henry IV and Champlain wanted to know why the early settlements had failed.

Champlain became increasingly curious about North America and had many discussions with the king about the possibilities for designing a new country that had all of the best attributes of France without any of the problems. In 1603, Champlain made the first of twenty-seven transatlantic crossings. The expedition was headed by François Gravé Dupont, whose main objective was to investigate the fur trade. The two men became lifelong friends, and Dupont taught Champlain many interesting details about the topography of the Saint Lawrence River, an area in New York State that we know today as Arcadia.

Champlain returned to North America in 1604 with Baron de Poutrincourt and Pierre Dugua. They established a settlement on Saint Croix Island in the Saint Croix River, which is nestled between what is now Minnesota and Wisconsin. The winter was so harsh that their small group almost starved to death. They moved their settlement to Port Royal, in what is now Nova Scotia. Port Royal became the base for all of their East Coast explorations. Baron de Poutrincourt journeyed south to explore what is now Maine.

Without fruits and green vegetables, scurvy was a major problem for the explorers. Those in some circles thought it was caused by idleness. Champlain did his best to keep the group occupied, which speaks volumes about his leadership skills. When Baron de Poutrincourt returned from his sojourn south on November 14, 1606, Champlain and his men planned an elaborate banquet and wrote a play about sailors who discovered the New World and met Neptune along the way. The baron was presented with a chain. The next day he put the chain around the neck of another, who in turn had to create the menu, source the food, and create entertainment for the evening. Thus, the rotation began.

November 14 is still celebrated in Canada today, especially in Nova Scotia, as "The Order of Good Cheer." In his book, *Voyages of Champlain*, published in 1613, Champlain refers to this occasion as *L'Odre de Bon Temps*.

Samuel de Champlain went on to become the founder of modern-day Canada, the settlement he and Henry IV called New France. By 1608, Champlain had established a colony on the banks of the Saint Lawrence River that is now Quebec. Forever the restless explorer, he was the first European to see the lake between the Green Mountains of Vermont and the Adirondack Mountains of upper New York State. In 1609, he named that body of water Lake Champlain.

During his explorations, Champlain often returned to France in times of political turmoil. He wrote extensively of his journeys and published several books and articles that were widely read in France. His last trip to Quebec was in 1633. Champlain received the title of Lieutenant General of New France. He died of a stroke two years later. Champlain was survived by his wife, Helene, who spent most of her time in France. The couple never had any children.

For me, one of Champlain's greatest legacies was the relationship he forged with the local Indian tribes. He sent young French boys to live with the Indians to study their language and culture. Champlain's respect for other cultures, acute leadership skills, vision for a better society, and determination contribute to his status as a worthy hero.

Monsieur and Madame Cabot

Request the Pleasure of Your Company to Celebrate

The Life and Times of the Great Explorer

Samuel de Champlain

(Unknown Date, 1574-December 25, 1635)

(date and location)

Please bring a historical fact to share. Period costumes are appreciated but not required.

rsvp (telephone number and e-mail address)

Caribou Cocktails begin at 7:00 pm   Dinner Commences at 8:00 pm

Table Setting

This detail was somewhat of a challenge. Champlain's banquets were held in the dead of winter in an inclement climate in the wilderness. Who knows if they even had forks? It was not uncommon for explorers to eat with their hands and pick up meat with their hunting knives.

So, there are two approaches you can take. Either give up the notion of having a table that reflects the period, or set a table that reflects the spirit of Champlain's experience. I used the latter approach. My thoughts turned to a table setting with a hunting theme. Champlain's greatest challenge was keeping his men's morale up while also feeding them. Cleverly, Champlain had each person in the group play host for one evening. That person would have to complete the hunt and plan the entertainment. It gave the men something to focus on and served as a distraction from their miserable surroundings.

My husband, Sam, has shot many deer over the course of our marriage, and we have accumulated myriad antlers. Some of these live at the bottom of our freezer, waiting for a prestigious mounting, which will probably never happen. We also have replicas of game birds. So, I used the smallest set of antlers I could find and covered the skull with moss for the centerpiece. I pasted a small feather on the place card of each guest. Mats seemed more appropriate than a tablecloth; in all honesty, if we had had a bear skin rug I would have gladly put that on top of the table! This was a great opportunity to use local native bushes and evergreens, which have a marvelous scent. Needless to say, Champlain and his men would have had only candles for light.

Music

Chances are that some of the men in Champlain's group played instruments. If not instruments, surely there were men with good voices. Sixteenth-century French music often had flutelike instruments call *flageolets*, which were made of wood and came in different sizes. There was also a wide variety of stringed instruments and horns. We found some sixteenth-century lute music on Amazon. The sound was gentle and pleasing, even if not totally authentic.

Menu for Eight

Caribou Cocktail

Hors d'oeuvres
Smoked Trout with Crackers

First Course
Country Pâté with French Bread, Butter, and Cornichons (a type of pickle)

Main Course
Roast Pork Tenderloin with Mushroom Gravy or Roast Venison
Stuffed Onions
Baked Acorn Squash

Dessert
Bread Pudding with Maple-Brandy Sauce

Recipes

Caribou Cocktail
Preparation time: 5 minutes

8 cups red wine or port
2 cups rye whiskey, rum, or brandy
¾ cup maple syrup
4 cloves

Mix all ingredients together and place in a large pan on top of the stove. Heat over a low temperature; do not allow the drink to boil. Serve warm to your guests when they arrive.

Chef's Note: There seem to be many different combinations of this drink, which is traditionally served at the Quebec Winter Carnival. Originally, it comprised warm caribou blood mixed with alcohol and was drunk before venturing out for a hunt. This drink has a high alcohol content, so help your guests be sensible.

Smoked Trout with Crackers
Preparation time: 15 minutes

8 ounces smoked trout
½ cup mayonnaise
Juice from one medium-sized lemon
Pepper
16 crackers of your choice

Combine the smoked trout with the mayonnaise and lemon juice. Toss and add any additional lemon juice and pepper to your liking. Serve on crackers.

Chef's Note: I have eliminated salt because it is usually added during the smoking process. However, it you feel additional salt is needed, by all means add to your own liking.

Country Pâté
Preparation time: 30 minutes (Best made a day ahead.)

4 slices stale bread
½ cup milk
4 eggs
2 teaspoons each of cinnamon, nutmeg, and cloves
4 teaspoons each of ground allspice and coriander seeds
1 pound chicken livers
1 pound ground pork
1 onion
2 shallots
4 cloves garlic
Sea salt and pepper

Preheat oven to 350 degrees. Remove the crusts from the bread, and cut into small pieces. Soak the bread in the milk for ten minutes. Beat the eggs; add to the milk and bread mixture. Add all the spices; mix well and set aside. Chop the chicken livers, and add the ground pork. Combine the meat mixture with the bread mixture. Chop the onion, shallots, and garlic, and add to the pâté. Finish with freshly ground pepper and sea salt. Place the meat mixture in ovenproof dishes. (These can be either two seven-inch by four-inch by two-inch, or one nine-inch by three-and-a-half-inch.) Bake for forty-five minutes, or until a knife inserted into the pâté comes out clean. Chill for twenty-four hours, and then bring to room temperature. Remove the pâté from the pan, and cut two or three thin slices for each person. Serve with good French bread, butter, and cornichon pickles.

Chef's Note: I love good pâtés. This recipe is best when made a day ahead. It is for a rather coarse, hearty, country pâté. It will keep for a week if carefully wrapped but does not freeze very well.

Roast Pork Tenderloin with Mushroom Gravy
Preparation time: 15 minutes (Marinate in refrigerator for five hours or overnight.)

2 2-pound boneless pork tenderloins
1 large bunch fresh rosemary
1 large bunch fresh thyme
freshly ground pepper
½ cup olive oil
1 cup red wine

Preheat the oven to 415 degrees. Wash the tenderloins and pat dry. Combine the rosemary, thyme, pepper, olive oil, and red wine in a large bowl. Mix together and add the tenderloins, turning them over several times to coat thoroughly with the marinade. Refrigerate the pork for at least five hours or preferably overnight. When ready to cook, bring the pork to room temperature. Remove the pork from the marinade, and discard the marinade. Place the tenderloins on racks in a roasting pan. Cook for fifteen minutes. Reduce oven temperature to 350 degrees, and cook for forty-five minutes. Cover with aluminum foil for fifteen minutes to let the juices recede, and then slice.

Chef's Note: Pork should be thoroughly cooked. Never eat a piece of raw pork. Trichinosis is rare in the United States, but it does exist. Make sure the internal temperature reaches 137 degrees and the color of the meat is white or grayish. Likewise, carefully wash all utensils that have come into contact with raw pork.

Gravy
4 tablespoons butter
4 tablespoons flour
1 shallot
1 cup button mushroom caps
15 ounces beef consommé
Ground pepper

Clean the mushrooms and peel the shallot; chop both coarsely. Melt the butter in a frying pan, and cook the shallot and mushrooms until tender. Scatter the flour over the pan; this will create a thick paste. Gradually add the consommé, and stir vigorously until you create gravy. Add the ground pepper, and transfer to a double boiler to keep warm until serving time. Pass in a gravy boat.

Chef's Note: I make the gravy before I cook the tenderloin and keep it warm in a double boiler. The more you can prepare your meal ahead of time, the more you will enjoy your own dinner party.

Roast Venison
Preparation time: 20 minutes (marinate for 24 hours)

1 5-pound venison leg
2 cups orange juice
1 cup white wine
2 bay leaves
5 cloves chopped garlic
¼ cup olive oil
Ground pepper
Sea salt
¼ pound bacon

Preheat the oven to 350 degrees. Create the marinade by combining the orange juice, wine, bay leaves, garlic, and olive oil in a deep bowl. Rinse off the venison, and dry with a paper towel. Place it in the orange juice mixture, and refrigerate for twenty-four hours. Several hours before cooking, remove the venison from the marinade but reserve the liquid. Bring the venison to room temperature, and dry with a paper towel. Rub salt and ground pepper onto the roast. Place on a rack, and cover with bacon strips. Roast for one hour. Remove from the oven, and cover with aluminum foil for fifteen to twenty minutes prior to carving.

Sauce
¼ cup butter
¼ cup all-purpose flour
Reserved marinade
Salt and pepper
1 cup white wine

Heat the butter in a frying pan over low heat. Sprinkle the flour over the butter, and add the marinade to make a rough, thin paste. If the mixture gets too thick, add a little more wine. Add salt and pepper to taste.

Chef's Note: Champlain's men would have had venison and wine, but most certainly they would not have had orange juice! I am taking a bit of poetic license here, because the orange juice adds such a nice flavor. Venison is healthy because it has no added hormones, but it is also lean. The challenge is keeping the meat surrounded by enough fat while cooking. Make sure you completely cover the top of the roast with bacon.

Stuffed Onions
Preparation time: 25 minutes

8 good-sized yellow onions
6 ounces good-quality bacon
½ cup butter
4 cloves garlic
2 cups bread crumbs
4 tablespoons blue cheese
8 sprigs parsley, for garnish

Preheat the oven to 350 degrees. Peel the onions. Cut off the tops and bottoms of the onions with a sharp knife to make each one level. Scoop out the insides of the onions with a melon ball scoop or knife. Cook the bacon until crispy, and drain on a paper towel. Cut the bacon into small pieces. Add the butter to a frying pan, and cook the onion insides and garlic until translucent. Remove the pan from the stove, and add the bread crumbs, crumbled bacon, and blue cheese. Place the bacon-bread-crumb stuffing inside each onion. Cook for twenty-five to thirty minutes, depending on the size of the onions.

Chef's Note: I stuff the onions the morning of the dinner party, cover them carefully, and refrigerate. When ready to cook, allow the onions to come to room temperature for twenty-five to thirty minutes, keeping them covered. They are very good.

Baked Acorn Squash
Preparation time: 10 minutes

4 small acorn squash
½ cup brown sugar
8 teaspoons butter

Preheat the oven to 350 degrees. Cut each squash in half, and remove the seeds and fiber inside. Place on a baking sheet, and put a little brown sugar and butter in the center of each half. Bake for forty-five to fifty minutes, until the squash is soft.

Chef's Note: Squash of all kinds originated in the North and South American continents and were staple foods of the Native Americans. One of the biggest problems Champlain and his men faced was the lack of vitamin C during the winter months, which resulted in scurvy. The acorn squash are so delicious at this time of the year and provide ample amounts of that precious vitamin.

Bread Pudding with Maple-Brandy Sauce
Preparation time: 35 minutes

12 slices French baguette
5 large eggs, at room temperature
¼ cup brown sugar
¼ cup maple syrup
1 teaspoon vanilla
1 teaspoon allspice
4 cups milk
¼ cup raisins

Preheat the oven to 350 degrees. Slice off nine pieces of a baguette, and chop them into small pieces. Place in an eight-inch-by-eight-inch, buttered, ovenproof dish. Beat the eggs, and add the sugar, maple syrup, vanilla, allspice, and milk. Pour the mixture over the bread, and sprinkle the raisins on top. Let this mixture sit for twenty minutes. Push the bread to the bottom of the dish to help it absorb the milk and egg mixture. When ready to bake, place it in a large, shallow pan, and surround the pudding with hot water, creating a bain-marie (water bath). Bake for forty-five minutes, or until a knife comes out of the pudding cleanly. Serve warm or cold, with sauce.

Sauce
½ cup melted butter
¾ cup white sugar
1 cup maple syrup
1 beaten egg
¼ cup brandy

Melt the butter in a sauce pan over low to moderate heat. Add the sugar and stir until dissolved. This will happen quickly; add one cup of maple syrup and 1 beaten egg. Stir quickly until the mixture is well blended. Lastly, add the brandy. Place the sauce in the top of a double boiler and keep warm until ready to serve.

Chef's Note: You can make both the pudding and sauce ahead of time and warm before serving.

Postmortem

My favorite insight into this period of French exploration was given by one of our guests. She commented that historians often say, "When the Spanish colonists settled a new land, they brought a priest. When the English settled a land, they built a town hall. But when the French settled a new land, they were quick to build a theater." This seems to capture the essence of Samuel de Champlain's ability to keep his men happy during incredibly difficult physical conditions, which he did with an emphasis on food and entertainment.

Some of our guests were blue-water sailors and identified with the areas around the Saint Croix River. One friend pointed out that Champlain explored our New England coast and actually reached the tip of Cape Cod—a fact that even many New Englanders do not know. Another guest's point that Champlain had gone to Mexico and the Caribbean early in his career started a rather exhilarating argument from the gentleman on my left. The fact was duly confirmed by a Wikipedia printout, and more wine was passed!

From a personal point of view, I have always been fascinated by Samuel de Champlain. My father, Alphonse Senecal, was born in Plattsburgh, New York, and was of French Canadian lineage. It was always family lore—rightly or wrongly—that our relatives were among the early settlers who came from Rouen to join Champlain.

There are many good books written about Champlain; David Hackett Fischer's book, *Champlain's Dream*, is an excellent resource. The story of Champlain's life is one of courage, wisdom, enormous vision, and outstanding leadership.

Some historians think that Champlain's exact birthdate has not been authenticated; others think he was born on August 13. However, Sam encouraged me to choose Champlain for our February monthly celebration because the menu is hearty and Champlain's life reminded him so much of the fellowship he shares with his hunting friends.

CHAPTER 3

March Dinner to Celebrate the Life of

Henrik Ibsen, Norwegian Dramatist

"The spirit of truth and the spirit of freedom —
these are the pillars of society."
~ Henrik Ibsen (March 20, 1828 - May 23, 1906)

Henrik Ibsen is considered the first of the modern playwrights and as important to the theater as William Shakespeare.

Ibsen was born in Skien, Norway, the eldest of five siblings after his brother died. His father, Knud, was descended from sea captains and was a businessperson who lost his fortune when Henrik turned sixteen. The only possession that was left of the family fortune after Knud satisfied his creditors was an old farmhouse outside of Skien.

Henrik is reported to have been a lonely child who liked to keep to himself. At school, his talent for painting began to emerge. His unhappiness as a teen was heightened by a rumor that his mother had had an affair with another man and Henrik's father was not Knud. This rumor was never confirmed.

Throughout Ibsen's work, he drew heavily upon his own relationships. His play, *The Wild Duck*, takes place in an old farmhouse, with much of the drama occurring in the attic. One of the characters, Hedvig, bears the same name as Henrik's favorite sister. Another, Ekdal, is thought to represent his father.

Ibsen first began writing during the straight-laced Victorian period, when a strict moral code prevailed in Norway and throughout Europe. He was the first playwright to discuss taboo issues such as marital problems, children born out of wedlock, and syphilis. Many Norwegians considered his work scandalous. Ibsen had enormous respect for women and thought they should play a stronger role in society.

Ibsen wrote a total of twenty-six plays and one poetry collection. His career did not start with instant success. His first play, *Catalina*, was produced in 1850 but was not well received. He spent the next year in Bergen as a stage director. In 1864, he moved to Italy and then eventually to Germany because he did not like the protocols of the Norwegian politicians.

Many literary historians divide Ibsen's plays into two phases. For the first twenty-five years, he wrote historical dramas, many of which were based on Norwegian folktales. However, by the late 1870s he was beginning to use his plays as instruments for social change. This was evident in his play, *The Pillars of Society*, written in 1877. It involves a wealthy, ruthless businessman who goes free despite being guilty of attempted murder.

Ibsen's subject matter and themes, based on his deep understanding of human nature, continue to be timely and meaningful. Many of his plays are still performed today, and several have been updated and adapted into movies. Ibsen strongly influenced many later writers, like Anton Chekhov and George Bernard Shaw.

Handwriting of Henrik Ibsen

Ibsen's script indicates a person with strong emotional reserve who was keenly intellectual. His thinking patterns were extremely analytical, and he was a cumulative thinker—a person who acquired and used knowledge in a building-block fashion, like a scientist. Ibsen was the type of person who wanted to have a plan before he charted his path.

Postscript

Norwegian cuisine is one of my favorites. My first introduction to it was at the age of seventeen, when I spent a summer on the island of Bjerke in the Oslo fjord. Norwegian food is as healthy as it is delicious. Sam and I took a marvelous trip to Norway, which rekindled my love of this country. We got a kick out of seeing small bottles of fish oil with little cups on our breakfast buffet table in the morning. Celebrating the life of Henrik Ibsen seemed like a natural.

Herr og Fru Samuel Cabot
invite you to a dinner to celebrate the life and times of

NORWEGIAN PLAYWRIGHT

HENRIK IBSEN

(March 20, 1828–May 23, 1906)

[date, time, and location]

Please bring a fact to share with the other guests.

RSVP [telephone number and e-mail address]

Table Setting

March, thank goodness, is in spring—time for a table setting that includes flowers. The striking design of the Norwegian flag features four red squares and an indigo blue Scandinavian cross outlined in white. The cross symbolizes Norway's faith as a Christian nation. So, setting a table using those colors seemed like a good place to start. I took a piece of long, bright blue cloth and ran it the length of our oblong dining-room table. Next, I took three pieces of bright-red cloth and ran them across the width of the table. I used white napkins and white candlesticks. In the center of the table, I placed a large, white porcelain bowl filled with white daffodils. Because daffodils are one of the earliest and hardiest spring flowers, they are noted for being symbols of rebirth and good luck. They are also referred to as Lenten lilies. Not surprisingly, the daffodil is March's flower.

Music

This part was easy. In 1845, Henrik Ibsen wrote *Peer Gynt*, a five-act play in verse that resembled a Norwegian fairy tale and dealt with procrastination and avoidance. He asked fellow Norwegian Edvard Grieg to compose the incidental music to accompany the play. Grieg's score became famous and, along with Ibsen's work, served to forge a growing sense of Norwegian identity in a country that had been dominated first by Denmark and then Sweden. The score is as dramatic as the beautiful Norwegian landscape of mountains and fjords.

Menu for Eight

Hors d'oeuvres
Beet-and-Goat-Cheese Baguettes
Pickled Herring, Plain
Pickled Herring, with Sour Cream
Crackers of your choice

First Course
Gravlax with Mustard Sauce

Main Course
Baked Haddock with Cream
Pureed Leeks
Cucumber-and-Dill Salad
Asparagus Tips with Walnuts

Dessert
Chocolate Cake with Whipped Cream and Strawberries

Recipes

Beet-and-Goat-Cheese Baguettes
Preparation time: 15 minutes

1 large baguette (preferably whole wheat)
2 ounces butter
1 15-ounce can sliced beets
1 8-ounce log good-quality goat cheese
Freshly ground pepper

Slice the baguette into eight pieces. Run the pieces under the broiler for five to ten seconds to brown slightly. Remove the bread, and turn each piece over. Cover each slice of bread with, in the following order, butter, a slice or two of beet, and a slice of goat cheese. Just before serving, run these under the broiler for a couple of seconds until the cheese melts. Top with freshly ground pepper, and serve while warm.

Chef's Note: It is easy to prepare this hors d'oeuvre ahead of time, up to the last stage of running the bread under the broiler. I have found that the best way to slice goat cheese logs is with dental floss!

Pickled Herring: Plain and with Sour Cream
Preparation time: 5 minutes

16 ounces jarred pickled herring
½ cup sour cream

Drain the herring. Place eight ounces in a pretty bowl on a large plate or tray. Mix the remaining eight ounces of herring with the sour cream. Place in another bowl, and set it beside other dish. Add your favorite crackers, and pass to your guests.

Chef's Note: True confessions: I have struggled with my conscience over this recipe because it has so few homemade components, and this is, after all, a cookbook. However, herring is a major part of Norwegian cuisine, and I desperately wanted to include it on the menu. Finding fresh herring proved difficult. When Marty, the gregarious owner of our local fish store, suggested that I go to a bait shop, I made the executive decision to use commercial herring!

Gravlax with Mustard Sauce
Preparation time: 25 minutes (Cure the salmon filets for three days)

½ cup sea salt
½ cup sugar
2 cups fresh dill, for curing
Freshly ground pepper
2¼ pounds fresh salmon filets, skin on
¼ cup fresh dill, for garnish

Mix the salt, sugar, pepper, and dill. Clean the dill but do not bother to remove the stalks for this portion of the recipe. Take a large piece of aluminum foil, and place some of the salt and sugar mixture on it; then place the salmon filet, skin side down, on top, and add the remaining mixture. Spread evenly over the fish. Wrap tightly, and place in a large, shallow dish. Place a weight over the salmon. Refrigerate for a day. Flip the fish over each day for three days. Excess water in the dish is common and should be no cause for alarm. Drain it off if there is too much. When ready to serve, remove the salmon from the aluminum foil and slice very thinly at a forty-five degree angle. Place the salmon slivers on each plate, and decorate with fresh dill that has been cleaned and had the stalks removed. Pass the mustard sauce.

Mustard Sauce
4 tablespoons Swedish mustard
2 tablespoons sugar
4 tablespoons dry white vinegar
1 cup light vegetable oil
1 cup fresh dill

Mix all of the ingredients together in the order given.

Chef's Note: Gravlax is the Scandinavian term for raw, cured salmon. In early times, salmon was buried in the earth, with salt as a preservative, during the winter months. Gravlax will keep for a good week and freezes very nicely. I also love it for breakfast.

Baked Haddock with Cream
Preparation time: 25 minutes

8 small onions
4 tablespoons butter
4 pounds fresh haddock
5 tablespoons flour
2 cups fish stock
1 cup heavy cream
Salt and pepper
1/2 cup fresh-grated Parmesan cheese

Preheat the oven to 350 degrees. Think of this dish as a casserole. Clean and slice the onions. Place them in a large pot with two tablespoons of water on top of the stove. Cook the onions over low heat. When the onions are soft, add two tablespoons of butter, and stir until the juices evaporate. Place the onion mixture in the bottom of a shallow, ovenproof baking dish. Place the haddock filet on top of the onions.

Now make the sauce. Heat the remaining two tablespoons of butter in a frying pan; when melted, sprinkle with the flour to create a roux, and stir. Slowly add the fish stock, and blend well. Add the cream, salt, and pepper, and continue to blend all ingredients. Pour the sauce over the fish, and add the grated parmesan cheese. Bake for about twenty-five to thirty minutes.

Chef's Note: You can prepare this dish up to the point of baking earlier in the day and refrigerate. Bring to room temperature before baking. If you don't have time to make your own fish stock, you can use clam juice. However, good stocks are really the secret of good cooking, especially sauces.

Pureed Leeks
Preparation time: 25 minutes

6 medium leeks
2½ tablespoons sunflower oil
½ teaspoon nutmeg
4 tablespoons sour cream
Salt and pepper

Cut the leeks at the top of their stems, where the stalk starts to turn green. Wash thoroughly in running water to remove any dirt. Place the sunflower oil in frying pan, and sauté the leeks over medium heat for fifteen to twenty minutes, or until the leeks are very tender. Remove the leeks from the heat, and allow them to cool slightly. Puree in a food processor. Return the leeks to the top of a double boiler, and add the nutmeg, sour cream, salt, and pepper. Test for seasoning. Serve with an extra dash of nutmeg.

Chef's Note: You can make this dish the day before your party. Bring the leeks to room temperature, and reheat in a double boiler for twenty-five to thirty minutes. If you have leftovers, add a little chicken stock and create a soup!

Cucumber-and-Dill Salad
Preparation time: 20 minutes

¾ cup good-quality white wine vinegar
½ cup sugar
Pinch of salt
¾ cup fresh dill
8 cups English cucumbers
White pepper (optional)

Mix the vinegar, sugar, and salt in a bowl; stir until the sugar is dissolved, and set aside. Wash the dill and remove the stalks. Chop the dill, and place in a shallow dish. Next, find a nice glass or china bowl you would like to bring to the table. Peel the cucumber, and slice horizontally. Place a layer of cucumbers on the bottom, spread a little of the vinegar mixture on top, and then scatter a layer of fresh dill. Continue this sequence of cucumbers, vinegar mixture, and fresh dill until you have used all the ingredients. Finish with a little ground fresh white pepper.

Chef's Note: For best results, make this salad at least three hours ahead of serving or even the day before. The type of vinegar is all-important. Some Scandinavians like to use cider vinegar, but I like white wine vinegar because it keeps the color of the salad white. If there seems to be too much liquid when you are ready to serve the salad, pour a little of it off. These cucumbers will remain crispy for at least three days. This dish is particularly popular in Norway during Christmas but is very good any time of the year.

Asparagus Tips with Walnuts
Preparation time: 15 minutes

2 pounds asparagus
2½ tablespoons walnut oil

¼ cup slightly crushed walnuts
Salt and pepper

Clean the asparagus, and cut off the tough lower stalks. Steam for about five to ten minutes, depending on the size of the stalks, and sauté in walnut oil. After each asparagus spear is well coated with the oil, sprinkle in the walnuts, and cook for three or four more minutes to warm the dish thoroughly.

Chef's Note: The size of asparagus stalks varies greatly. However, you should look for those that are straight and plump. The thinner the stalk, the sweeter and more tender the flavor; the larger stalks are meatier. Slender stalks require less steaming.

Chocolate Cake with Whipped Cream and Strawberries
Preparation time: 25 minutes

4 ounces semisweet chocolate (with 75 percent cocoa solids)
1 teaspoon water
½ cup unsalted butter
3 eggs, separated
1¾ cups slivered, peeled almonds
1½ teaspoon vanilla
1 cup heavy whipping cream for topping
1½ cup strawberries, cleaned and halved

Preheat the oven to 350 degrees. Melt the chocolate and water over low heat in a double boiler. Melt the butter in a separate pan. When the chocolate is melted, remove from the heat and add the butter. Separate the eggs, and add the egg yolks to the chocolate mixture. Pulverize the almonds as much as possible, and add to the chocolate along with the vanilla. In a separate bowl, beat the egg whites until stiff. Fold in the chocolate mixture until there is no egg white showing in the batter. Place in a greased pie plate, and bake for twelve to fifteen minutes. The cake should be soft in the center. Let cool before cutting. When ready to serve, divide the cake into eight pieces. Whip the cream and place a small dollop on top of each piece. Finally, place a few cut strawberries on each plate.

Chef's Note: This cake is very temperature sensitive. If anything, it is better to undercook it because it is supposed to be gooey. Most ovens vary, so try to be sensitive to your own. I have also found that really pulverizing the almonds makes a much smoother cake than just chopping them. This recipe is very good for people who cannot tolerate flour.

Postmortem

As a freshman in college, I read *An Enemy of the People* by Henrik Ibsen. In this play, much of the town's wealth derives from tourists who come to bathe in the natural springs. The protagonist, Dr. Stockman, discovers that the springs have been contaminated by a tannery upstream. He expects the townspeople to revere him for being honest, but instead they turn against him. The first step everyone takes is to discredit him. The modern-day correlations are striking. It is impossible not to think of that play when you read our daily newspapers. Ibsen's plays have long fascinated me because their universal insights into human nature remain timeless.

Several guests had visited Norway and enjoyed the country's dramatic scenery. Norway is one of Europe's richest countries, but it opted not to join the European Union. One guest believed that the autonomous spirit of Norwegians was typified by Ibsen, who championed strong, independent heroes and heroines who battled the outside world, often to their own detriment. A wonderful Norwegian proverb says, "It is better to be a free man in a small house than a slave in a big one."

The conversation then continued on to various Ibsen plays and a discussion about which was everyone's favorite. For several people, *A Doll's House* got first nod. The plot is complicated but emphasizes once again Ibsen's theme of moral conflict among the characters.

The closing remark, which marked a lovely end to a dinner with very gregarious guests, was from someone who had done her research. Ibsen had several strokes toward the end of his life, which rendered him unable to write for the last five years of his life. A faithful nurse attended him. When she told him he was looking much better, his last words were "to the contrary."

CHAPTER 4

April Dinner to Celebrate the Life of

Thomas Jefferson, Third American President

"Nothing can stop the man with the right mental attitude
from achieving his goal: nothing on earth can help the man
with the wrong mental attitude."
~ Thomas Jefferson, (April 13, 1743 July 4, 1826)

Thomas Jefferson was one of our most fascinating presidents; the list of his accomplishments is long. He was instrumental in writing the Declaration of Independence and was a wartime governor of Virginia, a minister to France, and the third president of the United States. He took office in March 1801 and was elected for a second term, leaving the presidency in 1809. Jefferson was also the architect for the University of Virginia. It is curious that his tombstone makes no mention of his governorship or presidency.

Jefferson was truly a renaissance man with many interests. He was, however, first and foremost, a farmer, a man who strove to be totally self-sufficient on his five-thousand-acre estate of Monticello. Jefferson moved from raising tobacco to growing wheat. He had a wide variety of fruit trees and vegetables, not to mention a pond with fish that could be caught minutes before cooking. He is well known to many Americans as our third president but is less appreciated for his mastery of architecture, music, literature, horticulture, wine, and religion. In fact, there really wasn't much that did not pique his curiosity.

Monticello is located outside of Charlottesville, in the Piedmont region of Virginia. It is worth a visit. As a farmer, Jefferson was insatiable in his quest to discover new species of plants and different varietals.

When living in France, he often wrote to his farm manager and asked him to send seeds to Paris. Jefferson also sent seeds from Europe back to Monticello.

Jefferson loved good food. He hired a French chef from Annapolis to train his slave, James Hemmings, to study the art of cookery. In 1824, the senator of Massachusetts, Daniel Webster, wrote that "meals at Monticello were served in half Virginian, half French style in good taste with abundance." People served themselves. (To find out why, read the Postmortem section at the end of the chapter.) As president of the United States, Jefferson is reported to have handwritten invitations for his own state dinner parties. He thought that because America was a new country, so, too, should our etiquette be less formal and more reflective of our democratic nature. State dinners were rather informal. Jefferson did not like using place cards; he wanted the guests to sit wherever they pleased. The English ambassador found this pell-mell seating arrangement so horrifying that he and his wife left the dinner party.

I tried to create a menu that reflected Jefferson's rural, southern background. Early colonists worked hard physically to feed themselves. Some of these recipes might seem fattening by modern-day standards, but getting enough to eat was a major preoccupation in the eighteenth century.

My husband, Sam, and I got very excited about this party. With each month's dinners, our capacity for thinking of new ways to celebrate increased. It occurred to us that period costumes could add some excitement. I discovered that you can buy costumes on the Internet, complete with wigs, for less than you can rent them! Little did I know at the time that we would begin wearing these colonial outfits for all of our Thanksgivings from that year forward.

Handwriting of Thomas Jefferson

Thomas Jefferson's handwriting reveals a man whose strength of character and achievement stem from his intellect. He had excellent powers of concentration. His responses to other people and situations were always tempered by judgment. Jefferson could have been described as friendly but thoughtful—a person who might greet another with a smile but not necessarily an embrace. He had an exceptionally brilliant mind, the type of intellect that thoughtfully explored and examined the evidence of any given subject or situation. Jefferson was patient in his explorations and wanted to weigh the pros and cons of any subject before drawing a conclusion. He demonstrated excellent attention to detail. He also had a good sense of balance between the organization of thought and the execution of those thoughts. Jefferson had good administrative capabilities and made sure his ideas were carried out. He was a high goal setter. Like most overachievers, Jefferson was decisive and led others with enthusiasm.

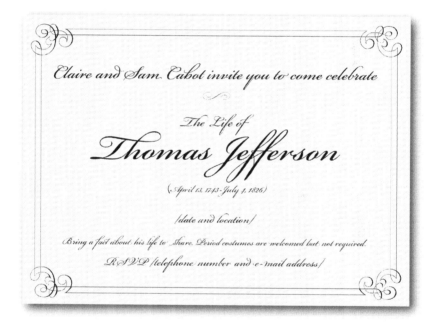

Table Setting

During colonial times, entertainment and socializing were centered in homes. This was especially true in the rural South, where guests often came for several days because of the distance between plantations. Quite a bit of competition evolved among hostesses to set as elaborate a table as possible. Jefferson loved simple elegance, so I chose place mats instead of a tablecloth. For the centerpiece, I chose two pineapples surrounded by apples placed on a large dish. Pineapples, which are native to the New World, were first seen by Christopher Columbus on his second journey to the Caribbean in 1493. They became a colonial symbol of hospitality, wealth, and fertility. Before long, pineapple motifs were being used in a wide variety of architectural details, china, and furniture. If pineapples are not available, you might consider red globe artichokes, which Jefferson also cultivated. I also put small, individual vases of alstroemeria (a type of South American herb) at each place setting, much to the horror of one of my guests. (More on that in the Postmortem. Do read on!)

Music

Thomas Jefferson played the fiddle. Music during this period focused on small audiences and dances within the home. The Internet is a huge resource, with many generous collections of music from the American Revolution and the colonial period. It was not difficult to find music. Your local library may also have selections.

Menu for Eight

Mint Juleps

Hors d'oeuvres
Crabmeat on Cucumbers
Cinnamon Pecans

First Course
Tomato Soup with Whipped Cream

Main Course
Baked Ham with Pickled Cantaloupe
Peas
Macaroni and Cheese
Ryland Cornbread and Butter

Dessert
Sherry Pudding Spice Cake with Peaches

Recipes

Mint Julep
Preparation time: 10 minutes

3 or 4 sprigs mint
1 teaspoon sugar
2 to 4 ounces bourbon or Rye whiskey
Enough crushed ice to fill a glass

Wash the mint, and separate the leaves from the stem. Put one teaspoon of sugar in the bottom of a tall glass. Crush the mint leaves with the sugar; then pour in enough whiskey to cover the mint. Let this sit for ten minutes. Fill with crushed ice and the remaining whiskey.

Chef's Note: This drink is very strong. Proceed with caution! Mint juleps were originally prescribed by an Englishman named John David in 1784 to be used by Virginians for medicinal purposes.

Crabmeat on Cucumbers
Preparation time: 20 minutes, a day before the party

16 ounces fresh crabmeat
3 tablespoons mayonnaise
2 tablespoons lemon juice
Salt and pepper
2 medium-size cucumbers
½ cup parsley for decoration
1 to 2 tablespoons Old Bay Seasoning (optional)

Place the crabmeat in a bowl, and break it up. Remove any cartilage. Add the mayonnaise, lemon juice, salt, and pepper. Set aside. Wash the cucumbers, and peel three long strips along the length of each. Slice the cucumbers horizontally and top with the crabmeat mixture. Decorate with a sprig of parsley or Old Bay Seasoning.

Chef's Note: Make up the crabmeat mixture earlier in the day, and construct the hors d'oeuvre just before your guests arrive.

Cinnamon Pecans
Preparation time: 20 minutes

½ cup sugar
2 tablespoons water
2 cups pecans
1 teaspoon cinnamon

Preheat the oven to 350 degrees. Place the sugar and water in a frying pan over medium heat on top of the stove. Rotate the pan back and forth until the sugar and water turn to an amber mixture; this will happen within seconds. Place the pecans and cinnamon into the syrup. Stir quickly, so the nuts are completely covered with syrup. Remove the nut mixture, and place onto a greased baking sheet; bake in the oven for ten minutes. Remove from the pan immediately and place onto a cool surface. Allow to cool before serving.

Chef's Note: Both Thomas Jefferson and George Washington grew pecans on their plantations. Pecans are the only indigenous species of nut in North America. You can add additional varieties of nuts to this recipe.

Tomato Soup with Whipped Cream
Preparation time: 25 minutes

¼ cup butter
1 medium onion, finely chopped
4 tablespoons flour
4 cups chicken stock
4 pounds of fresh tomatoes or
  2 15-ounce cans of peeled, crushed tomatoes
½ cup chopped basil
1 cup heavy cream
Salt and pepper
1½ cups whipped cream (for topping, optional)

Melt the butter in a large pot, and add the chopped onions. Sauté over low heat for five to eight minutes, until they are soft and translucent. Add the flour and continue cooking into a paste. Slowly add the chicken stock to create a soup. If you are using fresh tomatoes, skin them and remove the seeds; chop coarsely. Add the tomatoes, and stir vigorously to blend all ingredients. Cook for about ten minutes, and then add the basil. Blend well for another five minutes. Cool and place in a food processor. Return to pot and reheat. Add the cream. Adjust seasoning with salt and pepper to your liking. Blend well before serving. If you are serving the soup hot, do not allow it to boil. Just before serving, whip the cream, if using, and put a small dollop on each cup.

Chef's Note: I love this soup because it can be served hot or cold. You can make the soup, up to the point of adding the cream, the day or morning before. If it is a very warm spring day, you can choose to serve the soup cold.

Thomas Jefferson loved tomatoes. Some colonists thought they were poisonous, which is ironic because they are native to Central America and very much a New World species. New Englanders often used tomatoes for decoration instead of eating them.

Baked Ham with Pickled Cantaloupe
Preparation time: 20 minutes

1 6-pound bone-in ham
¼ cup whole cloves

½ cup packed brown sugar
2½ cups water

Preheat the oven to 325 degrees. Remove any excess fat from the ham. Carefully insert the cloves about one-quarter inch apart. Cover the ham with brown sugar. Place it in an oven roaster on a rack, and add water to the bottom of the pan. Cook for approximately one hour and twenty minutes (twenty minutes to the pound), or until the internal temperature reaches 160 degrees. Remove the ham from the oven, and cover with aluminum foil. Let the roast rest for ten to fifteen minutes before carving.

Chef's Note: The hams during Jefferson's era were heavily salted for preservation. Ham production in the United States has become very sophisticated. Many hams today come fully cooked and are served at room temperature. Read the label carefully to make sure you buy a ready-to-cook ham.

Pickled Cantaloupe

Preparation time: 30 minutes, at least a day before the party

4 unripe cantaloupes
1 quart cider vinegar
2 cups water
2 long cinnamon sticks
1 teaspoon cloves
4 cups sugar
5 8-ounce mason jars

Peel the cantaloupe, and discard the peels. Cut into small pieces. Set aside in a large ceramic bowl. Combine the vinegar and water. Bring to a boil, and add the cinnamon sticks and cloves. Pour the vinegar mixture over the cantaloupe, and store in the refrigerator overnight. The next day, pour the vinegar off the cantaloupe into a pan, retaining the cantaloupe. Add the sugar, remove the cinnamon sticks, and bring to a boil. Lower the heat to simmer, and add the cantaloupe. Simmer uncovered for twenty-five minutes. In the meantime, sterilize the mason jars with boiling water for several minutes. Remove the water, and fill each jar with the cantaloupe mixture. Screw on the caps of each jar carefully, and place the jars in a large pan with water. Boil for about fifteen minutes.

Chef's Note: This condiment is surprisingly good and just a little different from other pickles. They should last on your shelf for more than a year. Date and label each jar carefully.

Peas
Preparation time: 10 minutes

4 8-ounce packages of frozen peas
¼ cup butter

Let the peas defrost completely, and then sauté in butter. You will be surprised at how fresh and delicious they taste.

Chef's Note: Frozen peas are so good these days that I usually use them instead of fresh peas, which are not always available. We have gone on several tours of Monticello, and our guides always say that Thomas Jefferson loved peas.

Macaroni and Cheese
Preparation time: 30 minutes

1 pound macaroni
7 tablespoons butter
6 tablespoons flour
5 cups milk
1 egg
2 tablespoons whole-grain mustard
½ teaspoon cayenne pepper
1 teaspoon nutmeg, preferably freshly grated
8 ounces sharp cheddar cheese, grated
8 ounces mild cheddar cheese, grated
5 slices stale French bread
3½ tablespoons butter

Preheat the oven to 350 degrees. Boil a large pot of water, and cook the macaroni according to the instructions on the package. Drain thoroughly and set aside. Now make the cheese sauce. Melt the butter in a large pan. When it starts to sizzle, whisk in the flour and continue to stir. Slowly add cold milk. Beat the egg and add to the sauce, which will now be thickening. Add the pepper, mustard, and nutmeg. Remove from the stove, and add the grated cheeses. Stir vigorously. After the sauce is well blended, add the macaroni. Place in a large, ovenproof casserole, and set aside while you make the topping.

Chop the bread in a food processor until it is coarsely pulverized. Remove the bread crumbs, and knead in 2 tablespoons butter. Place the mixture over the macaroni and cheese. Place in the oven and bake for twenty-five to thirty minutes, until the top is nicely browned.

Chef's Note: The dish can be prepared up to the point of baking the day before the party; refrigerate and allow it to come to room temperature before baking.

Ryland Cornbread
Preparation time: 10 minutes

1 cup buttermilk
½ teaspoon baking soda, dissolved in ½ teaspoon water
1 egg, slightly beaten
½ teaspoon salt
1½ cups cornmeal
1 teaspoon sugar
2 tablespoons melted butter or bacon fat

Preheat the oven to 425 degrees. Mix ingredients in the order given. Grease a cast-iron skillet liberally with butter, and heat it in the oven for five minutes. Then fill the skillet with the cornbread mixture, and bake for fifteen to twenty minutes. Do not overcook.

Chef's Note: Getting the skillet really hot before you add the batter makes a huge difference in this recipe. Put a lot of butter in the skillet; cornbread gets dried out very quickly. Ovens vary in temperature, no matter what the manufacturers tell us, so test the cornbread after fifteen minutes. Cornbread does not freeze very well, but this recipe can be made quickly at the last minute. It is lovely served warm with generous pats of butter.

Sherry Pudding Spice Cake with Peaches
Preparation time: 1 hour and 25 minutes

½ pound butter
1 cup sugar
4 eggs
2 cups all-purpose flour
½ teaspoon each of nutmeg and cinnamon

Preheat the oven to 350 degrees. Run softened butter around a one-and-one-half-quart ring mold, and set aside. Cream the butter, and mix it together with the eggs and sugar; blend well. Sift the flour with the nutmeg and cinnamon. Combine the flour and butter mixtures, and place in the ring mold. Cover with aluminum foil. Place the mold in a large baking pan, and add boiling water to within one inch of the top of the mold. Cook for fifty to sixty minutes. Test for doneness by running a knife into the center of the cake; if it comes out clean, the cake is done. Cool and remove the cake from the mold. Either serve at the table and pass the peach sauce, or cut the cake into individual pieces and cover with the sauce.

Chef's Note: Pudding cakes were very popular in the eighteenth century. This cake is easy to make and very moist.

Peach Sauce
8 peaches, peeled and sliced
3 tablespoons sugar
⅓ cup port

Blend all ingredients, and let sit for thirty minutes or longer.

Chef's Note: Feel free to increase the amount of port and sugar. Taste and use your own judgment.

Postmortem
The visual impact of being dressed in period costumes was a big hit. Sam looked particularly handsome in his white wig. One guest described my costume as "frumpy," and my wig was so terrible I took it off during the hors d'oeuvres. However, it did set the stage for a colonial evening, and the laughs were worth being called frumpy. The observations and research of our guests have often sent us scrambling back to our history books.

I had forgotten that two of the guests were master gardeners and one was a landscape architect. One particularly acute guest looked at the dinner table set with Alstroemeria and said, "Oh, those flowers are all wrong!" She was absolutely correct. We visited Monticello the following April, and the grounds were awash in tulips and daffodils. Another very smart guest came up with the impressive fact that Jefferson planted 150 fruit trees on his property.

Our gathering would not have been complete without one native-born Virginian. An old school friend of Sam's boasted of having visited Monticello more than five times. His grandmother had, in fact, been taught by one of Thomas Jefferson's granddaughters. He was the generous supplier of his family's famous cornbread recipe.

Another revelation came when our native Virginian's bright and beautiful wife reported that Thomas Jefferson loved macaroni and cheese. Further research shows that Jefferson called all pasta macaroni. He even bought a pasta machine when he lived in Paris. He preferred pastas and vegetables to a heavy diet of meat.

My original dinner menu included spoon bread. My mother used to make it and I think, done properly, it is truly delicious. However, my efforts were disappointing, and the spoon bread was quite lumpy. After discovering Jefferson's love of pasta, I set about creating a good macaroni and cheese dish and eliminated the spoon bread.

Another marvelous revelation was that Jefferson did not like having his servants in the room during meals. The food was brought in and left on the table for guests to help themselves. One may speculate that Jefferson had such respect for his servants that he did not want them privy to the sensitive information discussed at the table, which they might repeat. Our English guest responded, "Oh, that is so typically American. The English would have thought the servants were too stupid to understand what was going on!"

Another brilliant bit of information from a guest was that Monticello is one of twenty-two World Heritage sites in North America. Jefferson's estate is remarkable and so beautiful. It is a must-see for every American.

My follow-up research found that Thomas Jefferson did not like having his birthday celebrated. Oh no, Thomas, I'm sorry! The only birthday he liked celebrating was that of the republic, the Fourth of July. He forbade his family to divulge his birthdate. As usual, we ended up learning more about Jefferson at the party than in our initial research.

CHAPTER 5

Ladies Lunch to Celebrate the Life of

Eva Duarte Perón, First Lady of Argentina

"My biggest fear in life is to be forgotten."
~ Eva Perón, (May 7, 1919-July 26, 1952)

Eva Duarte Perón was a fascinating woman. It is amazing how some people start with so little and accomplish so much, and others start with so much and achieve so little. Eva Perón died at the age of thirty-three. Her reputation may have appeared questionable to many, but she did overcome her biggest fear: she has not been forgotten.

Born in Los Toldos on the Argentine pampas, she was the illegitimate daughter of a wealthy landowner named Juan Duarte. Duarte died when Eva was six, and her mother moved to Junn, a larger city, where she supported her children by operating a boarding house.

From an early age, Eva possessed enormous drive. She was a beautiful young woman with intelligence, passion, and determination. She left high school after two years, at the age of sixteen, and went to Buenos Aires.

Eva was determined to become an actress. She had good luck getting small movie roles and radio parts. Eventually, she had her own radio show, called *Towards a Better Future*. On January 22, 1944, Eva went to a festival at Luna Park for victims of an earthquake in San Juan. There she met Colonel Juan Domingo Perón, who was the secretary of labor in the new military government. The two proved to be a powerful combination, filled with ambition and plans for a new order in Argentina. Perón was trying to elicit the support of the laboring class to make his own run for the presidency. *Towards a Better Future* gave Eva an excellent opportunity to promote Perón to the working classes. She was becoming increasingly popular, and people listened to her.

Eva and Juan were married in 1945. Perón was elected president in 1946. He would serve for three terms. Eva was a tireless voice for the working classes and especially for women and orphans. It was through her efforts that Argentine women got the right to vote. A law was passed in 1947, and women voted for the first time in 1951. Eva became very powerful in the Female Peronist Party.

She died of cervical cancer at the age of thirty-three but left a long and colorful legacy. Her romantic and stormy life was the inspiration for a Broadway show, *Evita*, the musical score of which was written by Andrew Lloyd Webber. A movie starring Madonna was later adapted from the musical. Even her sharpest critics agreed she could be charming. There are hundreds of books about her life.

Handwriting of Eva Peron

One of Eva's primary characteristics, which shows in her handwriting, is enormous passion. She felt things deeply. She would have remembered both painful and happy moments long after an event had passed. To her credit, she used her personal pain to better the lives of other people. This fact is particularly remarkable when you recall that Eva was born in 1919 into a class-oriented society with the stigma of illegitimacy. The size of Eva's handwriting also tells us that she looked at the big picture. She was conceptually oriented. Despite little formal education, she was quite bright and had the ability to analyze situations comprehensively. Her husband may not have gotten elected without her support. Finally, Eva's handwriting demonstrates an individual who was so self-reliant that she didn't totally trust anyone. This characteristic is hardly surprising, given her history.

CLAIRE CABOT INVITES YOU TO A
LADIES' BUFFET LUNCH TO HONOR
EVA DUARTE PERÓN
FIRST LADY OF ARGENTINA
(May 7, 1919- July 26, 1952)

Please bring a fact about Evita's life to share.
Come at noon, wearing something positively glamorous.

[DATE AND LOCATION]
RSVP [TELEPHONE NUMBER AND E-MAIL ADDRESS]

Table Setting

I could not find any information regarding the type of perfume Eva preferred. But looking at her carefully coiffed hair and bright-red sensuous lips, one would suspect it would have been a heavy scent. Our wonderful local florist was able to find some gardenias, which I placed in a low dish in the center of the table. I have some lovely light-blue linen table mats and monogrammed napkins that fit the bill. The scent of gardenia was most pleasing; I hope Eva would have been pleased.

Music

The choice here was obvious: the score of *Evita*. It is infectious! We all broke into song from time to time during our gathering.

Menu for Eight

First Course
Chilled Hearts of Palm Soup

Main Course
Matambre with Chimichurri Sauce
Roasted Eggplant and Peppers
Sliced Tomatoes and Onions

Dessert
Drunken Pears with Sugar Cookies
Iced Tea or White Wine

Recipes

Everything on this menu can be made a day ahead of time.

Chilled Hearts of Palm Soup

Preparation time: 20 minutes

2½ cups canned hearts of palm (approximately 20 ounces)
Chives
3 cups good chicken stock
1 cup half-and-half or light cream
White pepper and salt
¼ cup chopped chives for garnish

Drain the hearts of palm. They are usually packed in citric acid, which has a lovely lemony flavor, so don't rinse them before using. Place in a food processor and pulverize. Add your absolutely best chicken stock, and continue to blend. Finish by adding the cream. Add salt and pepper to your liking. When ready to serve, place in chilled cups and top with chopped chives.

Chef's Note: This is so good. It is best made the day before, so all the flavors have an opportunity to blend thoroughly. Invest a little time in making your own chicken stock (see chapter one for the recipe). It is the equivalent of going green in your kitchen, and the flavor of homemade stock is well worth the effort.

Matambre

Preparation time: 40 minutes. Marinate overnight.

1¾ pounds flank steak
4 tablespoons olive oil
4 cloves garlic
2 tablespoons vinegar
3 tablespoons lime juice
Salt and pepper
3 hard-boiled eggs
2 cups baby spinach leaves
1 large carrot
1 cup consommé
1 cup red wine
1 tablespoon fresh oregano
1 bay leaf
Twine for securing the rolled flank steak

Marinate the flank steak in a covered roasting pan in the refrigerator for twenty-four hours in the olive oil, garlic, salt, pepper, lime juice, and vinegar. Boil the eggs for 15 minutes; place immediately in cold water when you take them off the stove. Allow to cool before you peel.

Preheat the oven to 350 degrees. Remove the steak from the refrigerator, and let it come to room temperature. Do not clean the marinade from the pan. Cut three or four generous pieces of twine. Peel the eggs. Wash and dry the spinach. Peel the carrot and slice lengthwise. Lay the steak out on a flat, clean surface, and place the spinach along the length of the meat. Slice the hard-boiled eggs horizontally (easiest if you have a slicer), and add to the center of the steak, along with the sliced carrots. Now, carefully roll the steak lengthwise, and tie with string. You may need to call for help from another person. Return the steak to the roasting pan, and add the consommé, red wine, fresh oregano, and bay leaf. Cook for one hour and fifteen minutes. If serving cold, chill for several hours and then slice into half-inch thick pieces and place on a platter. Let each guest serve herself.

Chef's Note: Matambre in Spanish means "against hunger." I chose to serve it cold for this lunchtime meal, but it is also excellent served hot. When serving hot, allow the juices to recede into the meat for ten minutes before slicing. This dish is very colorful with the combination of green spinach, orange carrots, and yellow and white eggs.

Chimichurri Sauce
Preparation time: 20 minutes

2 cups flat-leafed parsley
2 tablespoons fresh oregano
4 cloves garlic
½ cup good-quality olive oil
4 tablespoons white wine vinegar
1 teaspoon sea salt
½ teaspoon ground pepper
⅓ teaspoon crushed red pepper flakes

Wash, clean, and dry the parsley and oregano. Remove the stems, chop the herbs, and place in a small bowl. Mince the garlic, and add to the herb mixture. Add the olive oil, vinegar, salt, and red and black pepper. Chill for several hours before serving.

Chef's Note: This is a delicious condiment, which you can also make with cilantro. You often see chimichurri on restaurant tables in Argentina and Chile. It is also an excellent accompaniment with fish and chicken. Chimichurri lasts for several weeks.

Roasted Eggplant and Peppers
Preparation time: 25 minutes

2 small eggplants
2 yellow peppers
2 red peppers
2 orange peppers
¼ cup fresh thyme
4 tablespoons balsamic vinegar
Salt and pepper

Preheat the oven to 425 degrees. Cut the eggplant lengthwise, and sprinkle with salt; let sit for ten minutes on a paper towel to reduce the water content. Dry off the eggplant. Wash the peppers and remove the seeds; cut lengthwise. Place peppers and eggplant into a large bowl, and add the olive oil and fresh thyme; let sit for ten minutes. When ready to cook, place the peppers and eggplant onto one or more large, flat pans (cookie sheets are perfect), and roast for seven minutes. Turn the vegetables over. Roast for an additional seven to nine minutes. Cool slightly, and add the vinegar, salt, and pepper. Cool for half an hour or overnight.

Chef's Note: This is best made the day before. I like to serve these vegetables in a long, shallow dish. The different-colored peppers make an appealing presentation.

Sliced Tomatoes and Onions
Preparation time: 20 minutes

½ cup onions
5 red tomatoes (Better Boy, if available)
4 tablespoons olive oil
Salt and pepper
2 tablespoons fresh basil
2 tablespoons lemon juice

Remove the outer skins from the onions and slice horizontally. Sprinkle with salt, and let sit for ten minutes; this takes the bitterness out of the onions. Slice the tomatoes horizontally. Arrange attractively on either a round or long serving dish. Add the onion rings on top. Add the olive oil, salt, and pepper. Let sit for another ten minutes while you wash the basil. Remove the leaves from the stems and chop. Finish by adding the lemon juice, and top with basil.

Chef's Note: This is a typical Argentine and Chilean salad. I have discovered that leaving tomatoes (which some people think of as a fruit) out of the refrigerator enhances their flavor. Just make sure to use them quickly before they spoil.

Drunken Pears
Preparation time: 25 minutes

1½ bottles red wine
1¼ cup sugar
1 cinnamon stick
8 firm Bosc pears (try to find ones that sit upright)
4 teaspoons cornstarch
1 tablespoon water

Warm the wine, sugar, and cinnamon stick over low to moderate heat in a large pot. Sit each pear on a flat surface; to enable them to stand upright, you may need to shave off a small portion on the bottom. Peel the pears. Stir the wine mixture to make sure the sugar is totally dissolved, and then add the pears. Cover and lower the temperature to a simmer for fifteen minutes. Turn the pears over so they are covered with the wine, and cook for another fifteen minutes (see *Chef's Note*). Carefully remove the pears from the wine, and set aside.

Now create the sauce. Bring the wine to a boil, and reduce it by one-third. Remove the cinnamon stick. Add the cornstarch to a small amount of water to create a thick paste; add to the wine, and stir constantly until the sauce thickens. Allow to cool. To serve, put a little of the sauce in the bottom of each dish, and add your upstanding pear. Knives are required to cut the pears easily.

Chef's Note: Poach the pears the day before the party, and let them steep in the wine overnight. Remove the pears from the wine, and make the sauce as explained above. The deep ruby-red color of the pears is very beautiful and seems so appropriate for a colorful lady like Evita!

Sugar Cookies
Preparation time: 15 minutes (Allow to rest at least an hour.)

¾ pound of butter, at room temperature
1¾ cups sugar
2 eggs
3 cups flour (and small amount to roll out dough)
3 teaspoons baking powder
¼ teaspoon salt
1 teaspoon vanilla

Preheat oven to 375 degrees. Mix the butter and sugar until well blended. Add the eggs and vanilla, and mix until well blended. In a bowl, place three cups of flour (reserve the remainder for rolling out the dough), and add the baking powder. Stir several times so the dry ingredients are evenly distributed. Add these dry ingredients to the butter mixture and blend. After creating a dough ball, wrap in plastic wrap or wax paper, and chill in the refrigerator for at least an hour. When ready to bake, butter a cookie sheet. Sprinkle a little flour on a clean surface, and roll out the dough to roughly one-quarter-inch thickness. Stamp out the cookies with a cookie cutter. (I used star-shaped cutters for my fabulous ladies.) Bake for ten to twelve minutes.

Chef's Note: I often wonder what we did before we had freezers, food processors, and electric mixers! I love making food when I have time and then freezing it. Cookies are a perfect example of an item you can make ahead and have in your freezer. Always label everything with the date. Even if you live in an apartment, utilize your culinary assets to the maximum. Cookies defrost within half an hour.

Postmortem

The Argentine flag arrived a day late. My secret desire is to meet an Argentine dignitary who we invite to dinner so we can display the flag. Oh well, as Robert Burns, our personality of January, once said, "The best laid plans of mice and men often go astray."

The ladies arrived dressed to the nines and certainly did Evita proud. I love the company of women gathering for a single purpose. It has been my experience that motivated women with a focus are a powerful force; that was certainly true of Evita.

The discussion of Evita was spirited. One conscientious guest had read two books about her. Just for fun, I looked on Amazon to see how many books have been written about Evita and gave up counting at eighty-nine. And just think, she only lived to be thirty-three! Much of our discussion centered on the role of women during the past seventy years.

The most interesting comment came from my friend who trained as a nurse and married a surgeon. She discovered that Evita had died of cervical cancer. The Pap smear was available in the 1940s in the United States, but not in Argentina. Evita's Argentine doctors thought she had appendicitis, so they performed an appendectomy. Juan Perón summoned a knowledgeable doctor from the United States who examined Eva—but while she was under anesthesia! Can you imagine? He did not want her to know she had cancer. So here was a woman who fought for women's rights—and was largely responsible for passing the legislation allowing women to vote in Argentina—who never met her surgeon. We were all incredulous. It was fairly standard practice during the 1940s to keep information from cancer patients for fear it would be too upsetting for them.

Despite all of the controversial beliefs surrounding Evita's life, many of which are probably true, you can't help but admire her drive and spirit. She won many improvements for the working class in Argentina and did accomplish her desire never to be forgotten.

When asked to do research about a personality, guests naturally gravitate toward their field of expertise. A person with medical training instantly wants to know how and why someone like Evita died at age thirty-three. The guests for the Jefferson party who were landscape architects and master gardeners assessed Jefferson from a horticultural point of view. As for me, when I think of a personality, the first thing I want to do is look at their handwriting!

CHAPTER 6

May Dinner to Celebrate the Life and Times of

Queen Victoria, Monarch of Great Britain

"We are not interested in the possibilities of defeat. They do not exist."
~ Queen Victoria, May 24, 1819-January 22, 1901

Queen Victoria reigned over England for sixty-three years. She is the second-longest reigning monarch in the world, after the current Queen Elizabeth II. At the age of nineteen, she became Queen of Great Britain and Ireland and, later in her reign, the Empress of India. The Victorian era marked a period of enormous British influence throughout the world. It was said that the sun never set on the British Empire.

Queen Victoria was crowned in 1838. England was a constitutional monarchy, but the preceding royals had lost favor with their subjects because of their self-indulgence and lack of caring for their subjects. Victoria did much to restore the people's confidence in the crown with her compassion for the lower classes. She ushered in a new era of high-minded morality and a British attitude of superiority.

In 1840, she married her first cousin, Prince Albert of Saxe-Coburg and Gotha. It was very much a marriage of love. Together they had nine children and twenty-six grandchildren, who would go on to marry into the royal families of other European countries. Queen Victoria was often called the grandmother of Europe. Prince Albert was a strong influence on his wife. He was interested in social change and improved housing for the working class. Both Albert and Victoria were very keen on education and insisted on compulsory education for all citizens. During the Victorian era, the land system was reformed to give more rights to small farmers.

In 1857, war broke out in India. The powerful and very rich East India Company persuaded the British government to step in and seize the entire country. Great Britain united the country and gave the subcontinent the universal language of English. Queen Victoria was declared the Empress of India.

The Victorian era was a time of great expansion and exploration. With that expansion came a powerful military force. Great Britain seized control of many countries, including Egypt, South Africa, Australia, parts of Afghanistan, and all of East Africa. The empire needed many of the natural resources found in these developing countries for their growing factories. This expansion was not without morality. England became the first country to outlaw slavery in 1833. The British Empire had changed during the reign of Queen Victoria and was a very different place by the time she died in 1901.

Queen Victoria is said to have loved the color purple best of all. Her second favorite color was green, which is a complement to purple on the color wheel. Victoria was a talented artist and musician. She could read French, German, Italian, and Latin, although she spoke only English. Queen Victoria was the first woman to wear a white wedding dress. Henceforth, any woman who could afford a new dress on that day wore white. We owe much to the Victorian era, which influenced architecture, food, and many of our attitudes. During this period, the middle class in England began to thrive. It was comprised of people with time on their hands, who could garden for pleasure, keep dogs as pets, and pursue other leisure activities.

A charming movie called *The Young Victoria*, starring Emily Blunt and Rupert Friend, is well worth watching. Not only does it give insight into Queen Victoria's painful youth as an only child, but it also gives a wonderful sense of the clothing, manners, and politics of the era.

Handwriting of Queen Victoria

Queen Victoria's handwriting indicates a bold and colorful personality. Her dramatic long, flowing T bars indicate a woman who led with enthusiasm. She had a sharp, analytical mind but she was not without a short temper. She had good skills when it came to the execution rather than the organization of ideas. Luckily, she had excellent advisors, particularly her husband, Albert.

Table Setting

The Victorian era was a period of excess. The dinner table was yet another opportunity to show one's wealth. Because Queen Victoria was the first woman to wear a white wedding gown, it seemed appropriate to use a starched white tablecloth and napkins. We have a wonderful local florist. I often go to her for advice about appropriate flowers for a given table setting. She suggested buying white roses that had slightly passed their prime. She instructed me to leave the roses in the refrigerator and, on the day of the party, peel off the petals of each rose and strew them down the center of the table! The results were magical. I followed through on the white color scheme with white candles.

Music

Nineteenth-century music was romantic and dramatic. Queen Victoria loved opera and oratorios. Her particular favorite is said to have been *Lohengrin*, the three-and-a-half-hour opera written by Wagner, which was first produced in 1850. She also is said to have loved Handel's *Messiah*. There are many excellent choices from this era, so it is a matter of your own personal preference.

Menu for Eight

Hors d'oeuvres
Cheddar-Cheese Rounds
Mushroom Caps with Cream Cheese and Smoked Oysters

First Course
Pea Soup with Fresh Mint
and/or Salmon Mousse with Sour Cream Dill Sauce

Main Course
Roast Beef Tenderloin
Mashed Carrots
Brussels Sprouts with Onions and Toasted Almonds
Mango Chutney

Dessert
Coffee Mousse with Chocolate-Custard Sauce
Walnut Peppermint Fudge

Recipes

Cheddar-Cheese Rounds
Preparation time: 10 minutes

½ cup cheddar cheese
½ teaspoon curry powder
3 tablespoons chopped onions
6 pieces whole-wheat bread
Butter (for greasing cookie sheet)
6 grapes, sliced in half

Turn on the broiler. Grate the cheddar cheese. Place into a small bowl, and add the curry powder and chopped onions. Set aside. Remove the crusts from the bread; using a two-inch cookie cutter, stamp out circles from all the pieces. Place the circles on a cookie sheet rubbed with a thin layer of butter, and place under the broiler for a minute or two to slightly brown each piece. Remove from the oven, and place a little of the cheese mixture on each circle. Place under the broiler for another couple of minutes, until the cheese bubbles but does not burn. Remove and decorate with half a grape. Serve immediately.

Chef's Note: You can make these just before your guests arrive, and keep them warm in the oven. Be careful not to let them overcook or get soggy.

Mushroom Caps with Cream Cheese and Smoked Oysters
Preparation time: 10 minutes

10 small button mushroom caps
4 ounces cream cheese, at room temperature
10 smoked oysters
4 tablespoons chopped fresh parsley

Wash the mushrooms, and remove the stems. Drain on a paper towel until dry. Hollow out the inside of each mushroom with a melon cutter. Put a bit of cream cheese in the bottom of each mushroom, and top with a smoked oyster. Arrange on a plate, and garnish with chopped parsley.

Chef's Note: There were references to cream cheese from Lincolnshire, England, as early as 1583.

Pea Soup
Preparation time: 35 minutes

4 cups leeks, including the green part of the stalk
¼ cup butter
3 10-ounce boxes frozen peas, at room temperature
6 cups chicken stock
½ cup chives
¾ cup cream
Salt and pepper
½ cup chopped fresh mint for garnish

Wash the leeks thoroughly, making sure to remove all the dirt. Chop each stem into small pieces, including a small portion of the green part. Add the butter to a large pot, and sauté the leeks until soft. Then add the peas, chicken stock, chives, salt, and pepper, and cook on low heat for thirty minutes or until all of the vegetables are soft. Cool the soup and puree in a food processor. When ready to serve, reheat in a double boiler and add the cream. Do not allow the soup to boil. Add the chopped fresh mint for garnish, and serve immediately.

Chef's Note: If you are making the soup a day ahead of time, refrigerate. Bring to room temperature before reheating, and then add the cream and garnish. Pea soup was Victoria's favorite. If you don't have access to fresh mint, you can easily substitute croutons.

Salmon Mousse
Preparation time: 30 minutes

Olive oil for greasing ramekins

3 tablespoons gelatin
1 can consommé
17 ounces canned salmon
⅓ cup grated onion
1 cup mayonnaise
2 tablespoons tarragon vinegar
¼ teaspoon soy sauce
2 tablespoons fresh dill

Grease eight ramekins with olive oil, and set aside. Add the gelatin to the consommé. Let sit for ten minutes, until the gelatin is absorbed by the broth. In the meantime, drain the salmon and place in a food processor. Pulse slightly, and then add the grated onions, mayonnaise, vinegar, soy sauce, and fresh dill. Heat the gelatin and consommé mixture in a double boiler until it is dissolved and in liquid form. Add to the salmon. Divide the mixture equally among the ramekins. Chill overnight. When ready to serve, run a knife around the outside of each mousse and place on the center of a small salad plate. Cover with the sour cream with dill sauce.

Chef's Note: This delicious mousse is very easy to make. I always keep tinned salmon in my larder.

Sour Cream Dill Sauce
Preparation time: 20 minutes

1 cup sour cream
2 teaspoons white horseradish
1 cup mayonnaise
1 cup fresh dill
½ teaspoon dry mustard
Juice of 1 lemon

Blend all ingredients in a food processor, and refrigerate overnight to bring out the best flavor.

Chef's Note: I love anything I can make ahead of time, and this fits the bill.

Roast Beef Tenderloin
Preparation time: 5 minutes

2 2½-pound beef tenderloins
4 tablespoons olive oil
Salt and pepper

Preheat the oven to 450 degrees. Rinse the tenderloins in cold water and pat dry. Coat the beef first with olive oil and then salt and pepper. Roast for twenty minutes, and then remove from the oven. Wrap the tenderloin in aluminum foil for twenty minutes. Slice into thin pieces and serve.

Chef's Note: Roasts of all types—beef, pork, and lamb—were served in middle-class English households for Sunday lunch. Members of the upper class, of course, could afford to have these roasts whenever they wished.

Mashed Carrots
Preparation time: 30 minutes

4 pounds carrots
¼ pound butter
¼ cup sherry (optional)
4 cups half-and-half or cream
Salt and pepper

Preheat the oven to 350 degrees. Clean and peel the carrots. Slice and steam for twenty minutes, until soft but not mushy. Place the carrots in a food processor, and add the butter, sherry, and half-and-half or cream. Season with salt and pepper, and place in a casserole dish. The carrots can be made ahead of time up to this point and refrigerated. When ready to cook, bring the carrot mixture to room temperature and reheat in a 350-degree oven for twenty to twenty-five minutes, until completely warm.

Chef's Note: If you lived on a farm in Victorian England, you might enjoy fresh vegetables like carrots all year long. Farmers had root cellars, which preserved vegetables by keeping them cool. However, if you lived in the city, you probably had fresh vegetables only during the growing season.

Brussels Sprouts with Onions and Toasted Almonds
Preparation time: 15 minutes

½ cup peeled, toasted almonds
1½ pounds brussels sprouts
6 tablespoons butter
¾ cup chopped onions
1 teaspoon marjoram
Salt and pepper

Scatter the almonds on a shallow pan, and place under the broiler for several minutes until they are lightly toasted. Watch them carefully to make sure they do not burn.

Clean the brussels sprouts by removing any outside dead leaves, and cut a small cross in the bottom of each one. Cut the larger sprouts in half. Place in ice water for ten minutes. Steam them for three to five minutes until tender. Plunge the sprouts into cold water again. Just before serving, heat the butter, and add the onions and marjoram. Stir vigorously until tender. Then add the brussels sprouts and cook over medium-high heat until warm. Sprinkle with salt and pepper. Scatter the toasted almonds on top and serve.

Chef's Note: I can honestly say that I do not like brussels sprouts. However, my dear husband loves them, and I think of them as being classically English. Picking the smallest sprouts and not overcooking them makes a huge difference in the taste. This particular dish is very palatable. The almonds add a lovely nutty flavor.

Mango Chutney
Preparation time: 1 hour

2 medium green apples, peeled and chopped
3 large mangoes, peeled and chopped
1 sweet red pepper, chopped
1½ cups sugar
1 cup chopped onions
½ cup raisins
½ cup white vinegar
⅓ cup finely grated fresh ginger root
2 tablespoons lemon juice
2½ teaspoons curry powder
½ teaspoon each of nutmeg, cinnamon, and salt

Combine apples, mangoes, red pepper, sugar, onions, raisins, vinegar, and ginger root in a large pot. Stir and bring to a boil over high heat. Reduce the heat to simmer and cook uncovered for about twenty minutes, until the fruit is soft. Stir often to prevent sticking. Add the lemon juice, curry powder, nutmeg, cinnamon, and salt, and continue cooking for another five minutes. Sterilize half-pint mason jars by pouring boiling water into them and then emptying the water out. Fill the jars to half an inch from the top with the chutney. Cover and boil the jars for fifteen minutes.

Chef's Note: You will have enough chutney for the rest of the year! If you are pressed for time, it would be totally appropriate to substitute Major Grey's Chutney. Major Grey was a British army officer who served in India during the nineteenth century and created this marvelous condiment.

Coffee Mousse with Chocolate-Custard Sauce
Preparation time: 25 minutes (Let set overnight.)

4 envelopes plain gelatin
8 tablespoons cold water
2 cups good-quality brewed coffee
2 cups evaporated milk
1 cup sugar
8 eggs, separated
4 cups heavy cream

Place the water in the top of a double boiler, off the heat. Scatter the gelatin on top of the water, and let rest for ten minutes or until the gelatin has been fully absorbed. In the meantime, brew the coffee. Add the hot coffee to the gelatin mixture, and stir until dissolved; set aside. Scald the milk with the sugar, and place in the top of a double boiler. Add the beaten eggs yolks and stir until the mixture thickens. Then add this to the coffee mixture. Add the heavy cream and continue to stir; remove from heat and allow the mixture to cool. In the meantime, beat the egg whites until stiff. Fold the cooled custard into egg whites, and keep stirring until you do not see any white flecks. Place in a large, oiled bowl suitable for bringing to the table, and refrigerate overnight. When ready for dessert, serve each guest from the bowl of mousse and pass the chocolate custard.

Chef's Note: Dessert was a luxury enjoyed mainly by the upper classes in England before Victoria's time. During the Victorian era this began to change, as Britain expanded its empire and food became more plentiful.

Chocolate-Custard Sauce
Preparation time: 25 minutes

1 cup semisweet chocolate morsels
3¾ cups milk
8 egg yolks
2 teaspoons vanilla

Melt the chocolate morsels very slowly in the top of a double boiler over low heat. Do not rush this process. Put the heat on low, and be patient. Slowly add the milk, and stir until the mixture is well blended. Beat the egg yolks, and add to the chocolate and milk mixture. Stir until the mixture reaches the consistency of heavy cream. Add vanilla. Remove the custard from the stove, and allow it to cool before refrigerating. When ready to serve, pass in a small pitcher for your guests to pour over the mousse.

Chef's Note: You can eliminate the chocolate custard and simply cover the mousse with whipped cream and toasted almonds, if you wish.

Walnut Peppermint Fudge
Preparation time: 25 minutes

½ pound of semisweet chocolate
½ cup sweetened, condensed milk
1 teaspoon peppermint extract
1 cup chopped walnuts

Melt the chocolate in a double boiler over low heat. Do not rush this process. When the chocolate is soft, add the condensed milk and stir. Allow the milk and chocolate to blend, and then add the peppermint extract and walnuts. Place the chocolate into a shallow, buttered dish and allow to cool. When firm, divide into pieces and serve.

Chef's Note: I cannot overemphasize how important it is to melt the chocolate slowly. If you have leftover pieces, you can place them in the freezer and try to forget the fact that they are there!

Postmortem
Sam and I like to get dressed up and have many like-minded friends. When I issued the invitation to one friend, he said enthusiastically, "Sounds like a good opportunity to get out my father's tails." The Victorian era lends itself to a total blowout, "put on the dog" dinner party. You can enhance an existing wardrobe in many ways without going to great expense. For example, I noticed that Queen Victoria often wore a ribbon across her chest. A trip to a fabric store would make that an easy accessory to create. Secondhand clothing stores or thrift shops are another wonderful source of potential outfits. During this period, tiaras and hats with long veils were in fashion. For men, top hats were prevalent, as were vests and bow ties. Photos on the Internet show men carrying walking sticks.

If you prefer a more casual style, you can celebrate the life of Queen Victoria as a denizen of the local pub. Queen Victoria loved sausages and plenty of simple dishes. For some reason I could not determine, she became a vegetarian after Prince Albert died.

Our guests had really done their homework, but one person caught me totally by surprise! She asked if I had prepared the meal using the same techniques as would a nineteenth-century cook. After a quick reflection on the menu, I realized that I used my electric mixer once and my Cuisinart four times. This food processor was first introduced in 1973 by

Carl Sontheimer, a retired engineer, at the National Housewares Exhibition in Chicago. Moreover, the entire meal was cooked using an electric oven, which almost instantly provided the desired temperature—without having to put more coal or wood on the fire!

It would be impossible to think of Victorian cooking without giving high marks to Isabella Beeton, a young woman who authored the book *Cookery and Household Management* in 1861, with the encouragement of her publisher husband. The book contained more than nine hundred recipes and tips on dealing with servants, treating diseases, and organizing the household. It became an instant success and is still used today. Even more importantly, Isabella was the first person to organize recipes with the ingredients listed at the beginning of the text. Sadly, after giving birth to four boys, she died of puerperal fever at the age of twenty-nine.

One of our very enterprising guests, an excellent cook as well, brought a lovely jar of Victoria sauce, which she had made from a recipe in *The Ball Blue Book of Canning* (ca. 1920s). The sauce was made from a variety of rhubarb created in 1837 by an English plant breeder named Joseph Myatt, of Manor Farm in Deptford, England. He introduced his new variety of rhubarb in 1837 in honor of Queen Victoria's coronation, which took place in 1838. In fact, this rhubarb became so popular that it spawned a rash of rhubarb desserts, considered a symbol of her reign.

Another well-informed guest shed light on the lengthy and complicated family tree that resulted in the placement of Victoria, an only child, on the throne at age nineteen. Her father, Prince Edward, Duke of Kent and Strathearn, was the fourth son of George III. He was the commander and chief of the British Forces in North America and the first English prince to visit America after its independence. Prince Edward died when Victoria was very young. Edward's three older brothers died without leaving legitimate heirs, thus paving the way for Victoria's accession to the throne.

The British Royal Family is famous for having dogs. This tradition was started by Queen Victoria. She had a favorite Collie, Sharp, who was named after one of her favorite government ministers. The dog, whose reputation was one of loyalty only to the queen, is buried in her personal garden at Windsor Home Park, Berkshire.

Of all the theme parties we have had thus far, this one presented perhaps the most creative possibilities. Queen Victoria ruled her country for sixty-four years. The options are vast for many different areas of study. We hope you enjoy your celebration of the life of Queen Victoria as much as we did.

CHAPTER 7

June Cocktail Party to Commemorate

World War II
News Makers

"You have enemies? Good.
That means you've stood up for something sometime in your life."
~Winston Churchill

It would be foolhardy not to incorporate at least one cocktail party in this mix of festivities. I was talking with my good friend Susie Bonner-Weir, who, along with her husband, Gordon, is a world specialist in the field of diabetes. She told me about a punch that her father, Dr. Tom W. Bonner, used to make. He was a distinguished physicist who developed important techniques in nuclear physics. During World War II, Dr. Bonner was asked by a Massachusetts Institute of Technology (MIT) lab to study radiation for the war effort. The scientists not only developed radiation but also created a famous punch, which they labeled "Silent but Deadly Radiation Punch." The story in and of itself was enough to motivate Sam and me to throw a party. It seemed fitting to continue with the World War II theme.

We have often talked about our parents' generation and their experiences during that stressful period. Sam's father was stationed in North Africa and then England. His parents wrote to each other every day, and some of these letters were read at Mrs. Cabot's funeral. My father was classified as ineligible from military duty because of his medical status. I have vague memories, along with pictures, of sitting beside a victory garden. My mother knit gloves and scarves for service members. Everyone in the country was involved and dedicated to the war effort in some way.

Sam and I are drawn to books and dramas about that era. As a young

woman, I felt there was a certain dour look—perhaps *gritty* is the word I am searching for—in the lined faces of our very tough-minded parents who survived the Great Depression and World War II. It was the generation in which people never spent more money than they had, took responsibility for their actions, and returned to build this country into the superpower it is today.

They also seemed to be a generation who loved wild parties. When my sister and I were cleaning out my parents' house, we found photographs of our parents and their friends at one of their famous New Year's Eve galas. One memorable picture showed my father with a woman's dress over his tuxedo and one of my best friend's mother dancing with a lampshade on her head. People in this generation also smoked and drank heavily.

In England, there was food rationing until 1954. That seems very difficult for Americans to comprehend. The 1950s was a time of growth for America. However, during the early 1940s all the best cuts of meat went to our troops. The US government hired people like Margaret Mead, the anthropologist, to teach people how to prepare lesser cuts of meat such as liver.

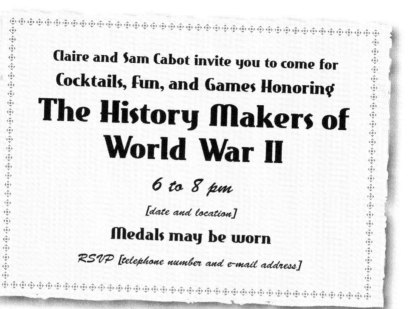

Claire and Sam Cabot invite you to come for

Cocktails, Fun, and Games Honoring

The History Makers of World War II

6 to 8 pm

[date and location]

Medals may be worn

RSVP [telephone number and e-mail address]

Table Setting

This was very easy. We set up a long table with a white tablecloth, a large punch bowl, wine, and liquor. Sam, a man devoted to his martini, was skeptical about the punch. However, he was pleased with the results of Dr. Bonner's recipe.

As I have mentioned before, I am a great devotee of secondhand stores. As luck would have it, I found a large cut-glass punch bowl in one of our local consignment shops. There is not a huge demand for these old bowls, and you'd be surprised at how easy they are to find. If you don't want to incur the expense, you can use any large bowl. Or you could wrap a big pan in brightly colored paper or cover it with aluminum foil. Years ago, I went to a party in Amsterdam given by some American friends who were stationed in Holland with First National City Bank. They served a World War II drink called a French 75. Young and budget conscious, my clever friend found a plastic bathtub and filled it with the gin mixture. After only one drink, the party became a success. Plastic never looked so good!

Music

During wartime, songwriters' lyrics are often about love, longing, and home. These sentiments are totally understandable. The World War II era produced some outstanding music, and we are particularly fond of

Glenn Miller and Tommy Dorsey. Playing their hits set the stage for our evening and game.

Sam and I went to see *The Glenn Miller Story* on our first date. He was fifteen and I was thirteen. The babysitter drove us to the matinee. Sam was the first boy to take me to the movies.

Menu for Twenty-Six

Dr. Bonner's Silent but Deadly Radiation Punch
Artichoke Hearts with Prosciutto
Curried Deviled Eggs
Spam and Olives with Mustard Dipping Sauce
Hot Crab Dip
Garlic Cheese Puffs Stuffed with Olives
Pickled Shrimp
Rolled Sandwiches

Recipes

Dr. Bonner's Silent but Deadly Radiation Punch

Preparation Time: 25 minutes (Exclusive of freezing the ice ring before serving). Serves 26 (4 quarts).

15 lemons, juiced to make 1 quart
5 oranges
1 wine glass grenadine (8 ounces)
2 cups white sugar, dissolved in 1 cup hot water
1 quart rum
1 cup Curaçao (orange liqueur)
1 quart brandy
2 quarts club soda

Juice four oranges, and slice the last one very thinly to float in the punch. Combine juice, sugar, and liquor. Just before serving, add club soda.

Mrs. Bonner added this note to her daughter at the end of the recipe: "Your father's policy was always to make the second batch weaker, partly because the punch is slow but potent and partly because the first cup, or two, is sufficient to make people happy and relaxed at the party and to get home safely. Please be guided by this wisdom." Laws governing driving under the influence have become stricter, so you might want to caution your guests to take it easy after one drink and, as the host, to be mindful of everyone's condition before they get into their cars.

Artichoke Hearts with Prosciutto
Preparation time: 20 minutes. Serves 18.

2 14-ounce cans artichoke hearts
6 ounces prosciutto
Plain toothpicks

Drain the artichoke hearts, and cut into bite-size pieces. Carefully wrap each with a piece of prosciutto, and fasten with a toothpick. Arrange nicely on a plate and serve.

Chef's Note: Do not use colored toothpicks; the dye often comes off on the food and is unappetizing. Make these the morning of the party.

Curried Deviled Eggs
Preparation time: 30 minutes. Serves 26.

3 dozen eggs, at room temperature
½ cup mayonnaise
2 teaspoons curry powder (optional)
Salt and pepper
6 tablespoons lemon zest
½ cup chopped parsley for garnish

Boil the eggs for twenty minutes in a large pot; remove from the heat and plunge into cold water. I often throw some ice cubes into the cold water. Let the eggs sit in the cold water for five minutes; this should make them easier to peel. Remove the shells, and slice the egg in half lengthwise. Carefully remove the egg yolks, and mix them with the mayonnaise, curry, salt, pepper, and lemon zest. Lemon zest is created by scraping the skin with a grater. Carefully wipe the egg whites clean. It is permissible to run them under cold water. Dry them, and fill with the yolk mixture. Garnish each egg with a little parsley.

Chef's Note: No one knows your guests better than you do. If you think some people won't be receptive to the curry, you can make half the deviled eggs without it.

Spam and Olives with Mustard Dipping Sauce
Preparation time: 20 minutes. Serves 26.

1 12-ounce can of Spam
1 7-ounce jar of green olives stuffed with pimientos
1 tablespoon whole-grain mustard
1 tablespoon lemon juice

¼ cup mayonnaise
Plain toothpicks, or there are some nice ones with twirls

Cut the Spam into small cubes. Put a tiny bit of olive oil in the bottom of a frying pan, and turn the heat to low. Fry the Spam pieces for a few minutes until they are crispy. Drain on a paper towel. Spear a piece of Spam and an olive with each toothpick, and place on a plate with the sauce in the middle. For the sauce, mix the mustard, lemon juice, and mayonnaise together, and place in a small bowl in the center of the plate of Spam and olives.

Chef's Note: This dish should generate a few laughs. Spam was created by the Hormel Company in Austin, Minnesota, in 1937. It is a canned combination of pork, water, salt, potato starch, sugar, and sodium nitrate. It was eaten often by troops during World War II. In many Asian countries after the war, the scarcity of food was a major problem, and Spam was highly prized. In Korea, for example, even today, Spam is considered a luxury and is often brought as a gift during the Lunar New Year. During economic downturns, Spam sales rise!

Hot Crab Dip
Preparation time: 20 minutes. Serves 16.

2 8-ounce packages cream cheese
2 tablespoons heavy cream
½ teaspoon Worcestershire sauce
14 ounces fresh crabmeat
1 teaspoon horseradish
4 teaspoons chopped green onions
Salt and pepper

Preheat oven to 375 degrees. Blend all ingredients by hand; please do not use a food processor! Place into an ovenproof dish, and bake for fifteen minutes. Serve warm with sliced, toasted French bread cut on a diagonal.

Chef's Note: You can prepare the mixture the day before or the morning of your party. Keep in the refrigerator. Allow the mixture to come to room temperature, and bake at 375 degrees for fifteen minutes.

Garlic Cheese Puffs Stuffed with Olives
Preparation time: Best prepared ahead of serving day. Yield: 48 small puffs.

2 cups sharp cheddar cheese, grated
2 teaspoons minced garlic
½ cup butter

1¼ cups sifted flour
Ground pepper
48 olives stuffed with pimiento

Preheat the oven to 425 degrees. Place the cheese, garlic, and butter in a food processor, and blend well. Add the flour and pepper and blend well. Put a little flour on your clean hands. Form the dough into small balls, and sink one olive into the center of each. Roll again, so the olive does not show. Place these balls onto a cookie sheet and put in the freezer. When ready to serve, remove from the freezer and bake for ten to fifteen minutes, until each ball is crispy. Be sensitive to your oven; cook until the balls are a golden brown. Cool slightly before serving.

Chef's Note: These are terrific to have on hand. It is quite fun to make them. You can also stuff them with nuts, black olives, or pickles. I always keep a supply in the freezer.

Pickled Shrimp

Preparation time: 24 hours. Serves 26 generously.

2 pounds (26 to 30 count) medium-size shrimp, peeled and deveined
2 tablespoons Old Bay seasoning
2 large vidalia onions, thinly sliced
1 lemon, thinly sliced
1 teaspoon celery seeds
½ teaspoon dried mustard
1½ cups cider vinegar
1 cup canola oil
3 cloves garlic
6 bay leaves
½ teaspoon sugar

Bring six quarts of water to a boil, and add the Old Bay seasoning and shrimp. Reduce the heat to low, and cook until the shrimp are pink. Remove the shrimp, and place them in a bowl of ice water. Let the shrimp sit for several minutes, and then drain. Combine the celery seeds, mustard, vinegar, oil, garlic, sugar, lemon slices and bay leaves. In a wide-mouthed jar or glass bowl, place alternating layers of sliced onions and shrimp. Cover and marinate overnight. Serve the next day, with small disposable forks or toothpicks.

Chef's Note: We are all used to having shrimp at cocktail parties, and they are always delicious—not to mention nonfattening! However, this recipe is just a little different and very good.

Rolled Sandwiches

Preparation time: 30 minutes. Serves 26.

12 ounces cream cheese
¼ cup chopped ham
¼ cup parsley
1 tablespoon milk
13 pieces white bread
13 pieces whole-wheat bread

Bring the cream cheese to room temperature. Combine with the ham, parsley, and milk. Remove the crusts from the bread. Smooth the cream cheese mixture onto a slice of white bread, and roll up. Do the same with the whole-wheat bread. Make sure you spread the mixture to the outside edges of the bread. Roll them up tightly, and place in a long, cylindrical dish. Cover and refrigerate for several hours, until ready to serve. Arrange on a platter, with alternating colors of white and whole wheat.

Chef's Note: You can mix the cream cheese with anchovies or chopped and seeded cucumbers instead of ham.

Biography Game

After everyone arrived and had a drink in hand, Sam introduced our friend and brilliant scientist, Susie Bonner-Weir. She told us the story of her dad and his work at MIT during World War II. Everyone was quite intrigued. Glenn Miller's music was playing in the background, and the stage was set for our World War II game.

Sam explained that we were now going to scotch tape, on the back of each guest, the biography of a person who figured prominently during the 1940s. Each person could ask another guest a yes-or-no question to try to guess the identity of the personality on his or her back. When each person had figured out who he or she was, he or she could turn the bio to the front.

Here is the list of the people we chose. We pulled up most of the information from www.biography.com. There are many sites on the Internet that can help you do research.

King George VI of England
Haile Selassie
Neville Chamberlain
Douglas MacArthur
Benito Mussolini
Franklin Roosevelt

Marlene Dietrich
Charles Lindberg
Charles de Gaulle
Amelia Earhart
Eva Braun
Francisco Franco
Dwight Eisenhower
Albert Einstein
Eleanor Roosevelt
Winston Churchill
Norman Rockwell
Juan Perón
Mata Hari
Eva Perón
Ernest Hemingway
George Patton
Pablo Picasso
Glenn Miller
Adolf Hitler
Joseph Stalin

We had one historical figure for each guest. I did have my doubts about putting Stalin and Hitler on this list. Both these men were pivotal to that era, but some guests might resent being labeled as either. Use your own discretion, by all means.

Postmortem

Many people wanted to know what we meant by "medals may be worn," which appeared on the invitation. We had had two marvelous, merry widows visit us from Scotland the month before our cocktail party. They both had arranged flowers for Queen Elizabeth at Holyrood Castle in Edinburgh. They told us about the experience and how lovely it was to work for the Royal Family. In appreciation of her service, one of the widows had received a gold pin from Queen Elizabeth. Sam and I were quite intrigued. We eagerly inquired as to when she wore such a commendation. The answer was quite simple: when an invitation stated, "Medals may be worn!" Because the fighting took place in Europe and the English set such an excellent example of tenacity, we decided to add this bit of British etiquette to our invitation.

We had invited good friends to our cocktail party but not necessarily people who knew each other very well. The game really facilitated interaction among the guests in a manner we had not anticipated. The most fun was watching a man whose personality was Marlene Dietrich. He just could not seem to figure out who she was. One of my old friends is a very good singer, so I encouraged him to go ask her for help. She obliged by singing Marlene's famous song "Falling in Love Again."

When I was writing up the notes for this party, I decided to interview one of our guests who was a bit older than I was. In all honesty, I was too young during that period to trust my own memory. Our friend Barbara said that her mother had come down to breakfast one morning and announced, "We will not use any sugar on our cereal." Barbara and all of her siblings graciously complied. "To this day, I do not use any sugar on my cereal," she said. The Germans were destroying all the supply ships, so sugar was very scarce. My friend remembers blackouts, when the windows were covered with dark shades. But she considered her family to have continued to eat well, even during the war.

One of our guests had the last laugh. We received a lovely thank-you note signed at the bottom with initials. For three days, Sam and I kept looking at the initials and then checking the guest list. Who on earth had sent us such a lovely note? We finally figured out that our dear, clever friend had written to us as his party persona!

CHAPTER 8

July Family Lunch to Celebrate the Life of

Nelson Mandela, First Black President of South Africa

"No one is born hating another person because of the color of his skin, or his background, or his religion. People must learn to hate, and if they can learn to hate, they can be taught to love, for love comes more naturally to the human heart than its opposite."
~ Nelson Mandela, July 18, 1918 December 5, 2013

Nelson Mandela was born in a small village called Mvezo, Transkei, along the banks of the Mbashe River. It is now part of the Cape Province of South Africa. His father was a chief in the Thembu tribe. Neither his father nor his mother was able to read; however, his mother was a devout Christian and took her son to be educated in a Methodist school. It was there that his teacher gave him the English name of Nelson. After his father's death when Nelson was nine, his mother took him to the Thembu regent, Chief Jongintaba Dalindyebo, who continued to educate him.

When Mandela was sixteen, he took part in his native tribe's ceremony for bringing young men into manhood. Chief Meligqili noted sadly that his people could not rule themselves because the whites were in control of South Africa. The whites suppressed the blacks and relegated them to menial jobs. This speech had a profound influence on Mandela, who eventually came to see that Chief Meligqili's words were correct.

Mandela attended church every Sunday and became a devout Christian. He always felt that Christianity shaped his life, and if you look at his many pithy writings, you can see the teachings of Jesus.

In 1939, Mandela attended the University College of Fort Hare. He studied English, anthropology, politics, native administration, and Roman Dutch law, hoping to become an interpreter or clerk in the Native Affairs Department. This was the highest office open to a black man. While at the university, Mandela was elected to the Student Representative Council (SRC). The students were very unhappy with the food and lack of representation in handling their own affairs. When Mandela spoke up for them, the dean of the college expelled him and said he could only continue in school if he left the SRC. Upon returning home, Mandela discovered that Chief Jongintaba was furious and insisted he go back to school and resign from the SRC.

After completing these studies and returning once again to his township, Mandela was told that Chief Jongintaba had chosen a bride for him. Poor Mandela was so horrified that he ran away to Johannesburg. He finished college through correspondence courses while supporting himself with several clerking jobs. He then enrolled at the University of Witwatersrand in Johannesburg to study law.

By 1942, Mandela was an active member of the African National Congress (ANC), a grassroots movement aimed at improving the lives of black South Africans. Mandela spent the next fourteen years campaigning for nonviolent acts of defiance. In 1952, with his friend Oliver Tambo, he formed a law firm to take up the causes of unrepresented South Africans.

However, the situation escalated. In 1956, Mandela was arrested and charged with treason. Along with Tambo, he was imprisoned on Robben Island for eighteen years. Mandela attained a law degree from the University of London through a correspondence program.

After a change in South African leadership in 1990, then-President Frederik Willem de Klerk released Mandela from prison. In 1991, Mandela was elected president of the ANC. By 1994, South Africa elected Nelson Mandela president of South Africa. He was seventy-seven. De Klerk was his first deputy.

In 1995, Mandela published his autobiography, *Long Walk to Freedom*, which he had secretly written when he was in prison. The book is a powerful account of Mandela's courage and strong inner convictions.

July 18 has been designated Mandela Day to promote global peace. Mandela is clearly an excellent example of a human being who tried to accomplish that goal.

Handwriting of Nelson Mandela

It was not surprising to me to see the characteristic of an independent thinker in Mandela's handwriting. This is a rare trait indeed, and one Mandela shares with Abraham Lincoln. When we, as handwriting analysts, use the term we refer to a person who may listen to others and seek their advice but in the long run does what he or she feels to be morally correct. Independent thinkers have a deep inner conviction of their own path. I very seldom see this characteristic in the general population.

CLAIRE AND SAMUEL CABOT

invite you and your family for a buffet lunch to celebrate

the life of

NELSON MANDELA

First Black President of South Africa

(July 18, 1918-December 5, 2013)

[date, time, and location]

RSVP [telephone number and e-mail address]

Please bring a fact about Mandela's life to share. Native dress is appreciated but not required.

Table Setting

Table settings for buffets are usually quite easy. Any colorful tablecloth will do. We prayed for warm, sunny weather, and the gods granted our wish. Because the buffet was informal and outdoors, we used paper plates, napkins, and cups but stainless-steel cutlery. I put up a large map of Africa with a star located at Mveso, South Africa, where Mandela was born.

Music

You can download traditional Xhosa music from the Internet. You can also find and share pictures of weddings and other celebrations. Almost all African music is accompanied by dancing and drums. Depending on the average age group of the party, encourage people to dance. This was not difficult for our gang, who love to perform at a moment's notice.

The soundtrack from the award-winning movie *Invictus*, starring Morgan Freeman, is another idea. This film describes how Mandela, recently elected president, wanted to bind the country together. He did so by encouraging the captain of the South African rugby team to win the world championship by beating the New Zealand All Blacks. The movie gives you a real feel for life in South Africa and is well worth watching.

South African Blessing

"A person is a person through other persons." This blessing was first introduced to our family by Naomi Tutu Sievers, the daughter of Bishop Desmond Tutu, the South African social rights advocate. She gave the graduation address at The Williams School in New London, Connecticut, where my daughter attended high school. Naomi explained that one large bowl of food is placed before all the children, and this blessing signals to the older children that they must take care of and protect the younger ones.

Menu for Ten: Five Adults and Five Children

Soup
Kaltschale

Buffet
Pickled Fish
South African Chutney Chicken
Sosaties (Lamb Skewers)
Geelrys (Yellow Rice with Raisins)
Green Mealie Bread

For Children under Age Ten
Peanut Butter and Jam Sandwiches

Dessert
Spice Cookies
Strawberry Tart

Recipes

Kaltschale

Preparation Time: 20 minutes (Make a day ahead of the party.)

10 pieces pumpernickel or other hearty bread
1 cup raisins
4 tablespoons sugar
2 teaspoons grated lemon peel
2 teaspoons lemon juice
1 teaspoon cinnamon
½ teaspoon allspice
3 quarts buttermilk
1½ teaspoon nutmeg

Toast the pumpernickel bread, and break up into pieces. Pulse in a food processor until it has broken down into bread crumbs. Meanwhile, cover the raisins with boiling water, and let sit for five minutes. Drain the raisins, and place in the food processor. Add the sugar, lemon peel, lemon juice, cinnamon, and allspice; process thoroughly. Add the buttermilk slowly. Chill the soup overnight, and serve in small cups with a little nutmeg on top.

Chef's Note: This is a great opportunity to talk with the younger generation about trying foods from foreign countries. It highlights a new approach to understanding different cultures.

Pickled Fish

Preparation time: 25 minutes (Marinate for several days.)

2 pounds cod or halibut
¾ cup peanut oil
3 large onions
½ cup brown sugar
3 tablespoons curry powder
1 tablespoon freshly chopped ginger
2 large bay leaves
1 teaspoon coriander
2 teaspoons sea salt
Freshly ground pepper
2½ cups malt vinegar
1 loaf sliced french bread

Wash the fish, and dry on paper towels. Heat half a cup of the oil on medium-high heat in a large frying pan or, preferably, an electric frying pan. Add the fish, and cook for four or five minutes on each side. It does not matter if the fish breaks up into small pieces. Remove the fish from the heat, and place in a large glass bowl. Scrape the frying pan clean.

Now, prepare the marinade. Remove the skins from the onions, and cut into small pieces. Add the remaining oil to the frying pan, and cook the onions until translucent. This will probably take five to six minutes. Do not let them burn. Add the sugar, curry, ginger root, bay leaves, coriander, salt, and pepper. Stir over low heat for several minutes, and add the vinegar. Cover the frying pan, and simmer for another six minutes. Pour this mixture over the fish, and turn the fish over in the marinade. Refrigerate and let the dish cure for several days. When ready to serve, place the pickled fish on the buffet table with pieces of freshly cut French bread.

Chef's Note: This dish may not appeal to the small fry, but it is truly delicious and worth the effort.

South African Chutney Chicken
Preparation time: 25 minutes (Marinate overnight.)

14 chicken thighs
2 cups yogurt
1 teaspoon cinnamon
¼ to ½ cup olive oil
2 cups chopped onions
2 cloves garlic
¾ cup mango chutney
½ cup mayonnaise
2 tablespoons Worcestershire sauce
salt and pepper

Marinate the chicken in the yogurt and cinnamon overnight. When ready to start cooking, preheat the oven to 350 degrees. Rinse the yogurt from the chicken, and dry on a paper towel. Heat half the oil, and fry the chicken until the outside is nicely browned. Place into a large, ovenproof baking dish.

In the remaining oil, cook the onions and garlic until translucent. Add the chutney, mayonnaise, Worcestershire sauce, salt, and pepper. Mix well, and simmer for a few minutes. Pour this mixture over the chicken, and bake uncovered in the oven for forty minutes.

Chef's Note: This is an easy dish to make. You can cook it earlier in the day, and reheat it for twenty minutes, covered.

Sosaties (Lamb Skewers)
Preparation Time: 25 minutes (Marinate a day ahead.)

4 pounds boneless leg of lamb
3 cups chopped onions
2 tablespoons curry powder
2 teaspoons ground coriander
1 teaspoon turmeric
1 cup lemon juice
2 tablespoons brown sugar
4 bay leaves
3 large cloves garlic
Salt and pepper
2 to 3 large onions for threading on skewers
½ pound bacon
12 skewers

Cut the lamb into small cubes that are substantial enough to thread on a skewer. Place the lamb in a large bowl, and add the chopped onions, curry, coriander, turmeric, lemon juice, brown sugar, bay leaves, garlic, salt, and pepper. Turn the meat over several times to coat it evenly in marinade; store overnight in the refrigerator. Remove the meat half an hour before cooking. Peel the onions, and cut into manageable pieces. Cut each piece of bacon into thirds.

Now begin threading the skewers. Alternate pieces of lamb, bacon, and onion until you have filled the skewer. Place these on a grill or under the broiler, and cook for about four minutes on each side. Grills vary in temperature depending on type, so use your own judgment.

Chef's Note: This process is time consuming. You can set up bowls with the lamb, onions, and bacon and get your guests to thread their own skewers, or make them up in the morning before your guests arrive.

Geerlys (Yellow Rice with Raisins)
Preparation time: 25 minutes

4 tablespoons butter or peanut oil
2 cups uncooked long-grain rice
4 cups boiling water

1 teaspoon turmeric
1 teaspoon saffron
2 teaspoons salt
1 cup raisins
2 pieces cinnamon stick

Melt the butter or oil in a frying pan over moderate heat. Add the rice, and stir until each grain is coated with oil. Do not allow the rice to burn. Add the water, turmeric, saffron, salt, and raisins, and bring to a boil. Add the cinnamon stick, cover, and simmer for twenty minutes. Remove from the heat; keep the cover on and let the rice sit for fifteen minutes before serving.

Chef's Note: Saffron has become more expensive than gold. Some supermarkets keep it under lock and key. If you are budget conscious and want to omit that ingredient, it will not be the end of the world.

Green Mealie Bread (Corn Pudding)
Preparation time: 25 minutes. Serves 12.

4 eggs
3 cups fresh corn kernels or 6 cups frozen corn, defrosted
4 tablespoons butter, melted
2 tablespoons sugar
2 cups all-purpose white flour
3 teaspoons double-acting baking powder
½ teaspoon salt

Preheat the oven to 350 degrees. Grease one bread pan (preferably ceramic). Beat the eggs in a food processor. Add two cups of corn kernels and the melted butter. Pulse several times to break up the kernels but not totally pulverize them; set aside. Mix the sugar, flour, baking powder, and salt together, and sift once. Pour the egg mixture from the food processor into a large bowl. Blend in the flour mixture, and then add the remaining cup of corn kernels. Place in the bread pan, and bake for fifty to fifty-five minutes. This is dense bread. It is important not to overcook it.

Chef's Note: You can make the pudding earlier in the day. Some people like to slice the pudding in a little butter and refry each piece. However, I would rather be with my guests.

Peanut Butter and Jam Sandwiches
Preparation time: 10 minutes. Serves 8.

1 loaf sliced whole-wheat bread or white bread

1 cup peanut butter
1 cup strawberry jam

Discard the first and last pieces of bread in the loaf. Spread peanut butter on one slice and jam onto the other slice; join. Remove the crusts, and cut into a variety of geometric shapes.

Chef's Note: Honestly, you will be surprised by how many adults will eat these.

Spice Cookies
Preparation time: 20 minutes (Bake in several batches.). Serves 12 (about 30 cookies).

2¼ cups all-purpose flour
1 teaspoon baking soda
1 teaspoon cinnamon
½ teaspoon ginger
½ teaspoon allspice
¼ teaspoon salt
5 tablespoons softened butter
1¼ cups dark-brown sugar
1 egg
¼ cup sweet sherry or port
30 whole almonds
1 egg white combined with 2 teaspoons water

Preheat the oven to 350 degrees. Sift two cups of the flour. Mix the baking soda, cinnamon, ginger, allspice, and salt, and add the sifted flour; set aside. Cream the butter, sugar, and egg in a separate bowl, and blend vigorously. Add the flour mixture in small batches to the butter and egg mixture until well blended. Add the sherry or port. When the dough has blended well enough to form a large ball, knead for a few minutes and place in the refrigerator for at least an hour. When ready to cook, sprinkle a little flour on a clean surface. Roll out, and cut with a two-inch cookie cutter or juice glass turned upside down. Place on a cookie sheet, and press one whole almond into each cookie. Whip the egg white with water vigorously, and brush a little of this glaze over each cookie; bake for fifteen minutes.

Chef's Note: These cookies keep very well. They can be made ahead of time and frozen if wrapped carefully.

Strawberry Tart

Preparation time: 45 to 50 minutes. Serves 12 generously.

Bottom Pastry
1⅓ cup all-purpose flour
6 tablespoons cornstarch
1 teaspoon baking powder
2 tablespoons confectioners' sugar
1 teaspoon vanilla
¾ cup soft butter
6 ounces strawberry jam

Make the bottom crust pastry first. Preheat the oven to 350 degrees. Mix the flour, cornstarch, baking powder, and confectioners' sugar, and sift once. Add the butter and vanilla, and knead into a ball. Roll out the ball of dough, and place on a thirteen-inch by nine-inch baking sheet. Use the back of your hand to smooth out the pastry. This will take a little patience, but keep at it. Prick the pastry with a fork on the bottom. Bake for twelve minutes. Remove from the oven, and cool slightly. Heat the jam for a few minutes over low heat, pass it through a sieve, and spread on the bottom pastry. Keep the oven turned on.

Sponge Top
4 eggs
4 teaspoons hot water
½ cup sugar
1½ cups flour
1 teaspoon baking powder
3 tablespoons cornstarch

Beat the eggs with the hot water vigorously until they are foamy, usually about one minute. Sprinkle the sugar into the egg mixture, and continue beating for another minute. Mix the flour, baking powder, and cornstarch, and sift. Add this to the egg mixture a little bit at a time. Beat for several minutes to ensure that the batter is well mixed. Spread this mixture over the pastry, and return it to the oven. Bake for another fifteen minutes. Remove from the oven and cool.

Topping
1 pound fresh strawberries
½ cup confectioners' sugar
4 teaspoons arrowroot
3 teaspoons sugar

Wash the strawberries, remove the stems, and cut in half. Cover with the confectioners' sugar, and let sit for fifteen minutes. Drain the strawberries, capturing the juice. Add enough water to the juice to make two and one-half cups. Add a little of the arrowroot into this solution. When dissolved, add the sugar. Place this mixture on the stove, and bring to a quick boil until it becomes clear. Cool slightly. Decorate the top of the tart with the strawberries, and pour the sugar water over them to create a glaze. You are now ready to serve!

Chef's Note: This sounds more complicated than it is. Just follow the directions section by section, and you won't have a problem. The younger kids loved this.

Postmortem

In Mandela's book *Long Walk to Freedom*, he describes times in his life when, as a student, he ate only one or two meals a week. That seems shocking, particularly given the amount of food in this buffet. However, this event can provide an opportunity to discuss the fact that not everyone in the world has enough food to eat daily. This is also an opportunity to explore how different people eat different types of food.

One of the young boys at the party announced that Mandela had made his last public appearance at the World Cup Games in 2010. Many of the guests had seen the movie *Invictus*, mentioned earlier, which was directed by Clint Eastwood. Matt Damon plays Francois Pienaar, the captain of the Springboks, a nickname for the South African national rugby union team. In the film, Mandela wants Pienaar to unite South Africa through sports by winning the World Cup. Against all odds, the Springboks, South Africa's team, win. The title of the movie comes from a poem by an Englishman named William Ernest Henley. The two opening lines in the movie are the last two lines of the poem: "I am the master of my fate: I am the captain of my soul."

One of the adults asked the members of the younger generation what they might do to make the world a better place. We got some terrific answers: Provide shelter for the poor. Plant more mango trees. Adopt a foster child. Provide better education for everyone. Clean up the trash on the beach. And, last but not least, encourage people to ride their bikes instead of driving a car to work. One of the other adults suggested we meet next year and think of a civic project we could all do in honor of Mandela. We loved that idea.

CHAPTER 9

August Dinner to Celebrate the Life of

Cleopatra VII, Queen of Egypt

All strange and terrible events are welcome,
but comforts we despise.
~Cleopatra VII, late 69 BC-August 12, 30 BC

Rarely has there been a woman more fascinating than Cleopatra VII, known simply through the ages as Cleopatra. The last member of the Ptolemaic dynasty, a family of Greeks originated in Macedonia, Cleopatra was smart, ambitious, clever, and sexy. She came to the throne at the age of eighteen and ruled for twenty-two years, ending her own life at age thirty-eight. The study of her life gives enormous insight into an era before the birth of Jesus Christ. She was born sometime late in 69 BC. Her mother was the sister or cousin of her father, Ptolemy XII, known as Auletes, who was a descendant of one of Alexander the Great's generals.

To thoroughly understand Cleopatra's motivations, it is important to comprehend the political climate around the Mediterranean region at the time. Egypt and Rome enjoyed a symbolic relationship. The Roman military leaders were very powerful. Cleopatra's father, Auletes, curried Roman favor to stay in power. When you understand that Cleopatra learned this lesson well from her father, you can better grasp her motivation as the Queen of Egypt.

During this pre-Christian and pre-Islamic period, Egyptian women were educated. They could read, own property, get divorced, and conduct many of their own affairs. Cleopatra embraced all of these freedoms. However, she broke with her Ptolemaic family tradition of speaking only Greek and learned Egyptian. In fact, Cleopatra was gifted linguistically and spoke many other Mediterranean languages. Cassius Dio, the Roman consul and historian who wrote in Greek, recorded that Cleopatra had an enormous ability to speak with anyone and make them feel comfortable. Cassius also purported that Cleopatra had a lovely voice.

When her father died in 51 BC, Cleopatra became heir to the throne and had to marry her ten-year-old brother, which was the custom. The next three years were tumultuous. Egypt was beleaguered by famines and political turmoil. Cleopatra's brother, Ptolemy XIII, was no match for his ambitious sister. She began eliminating Ptolemy's name from official documents and put only her image on coins. At the age of thirteen, her brother sought the help of a Roman legion headed by Aulus Gabinius. This legion, which consisted of five hundred men, had been in Egypt long enough to form close attachments to the Egyptians. Many of the men had married Egyptian wives and adopted their customs, so their desire to fight dwindled. In 48 BC, the Roman governor of Syria, Marcus Calpurnius Bibulus, sent his two sons to Egypt to order the Gabiniani (Roman soldiers) to come to Syria and help fight the Parthians. The Gabiniani didn't want to go, so they murdered Bibulus's sons. Cleopatra apprehended the murderers, thus ensuring the rage of the Gabiniani, who then backed Cleopatra's thirteen-year-old brother. This infuriated Caesar, who considered the legion lacking in discipline but also considered them part of his army.

Cleopatra needed the support of Caesar to stay in power. Several stories tell of her hiding in a rolled-up rug when Caesar arrived in Alexandria. However, the most reliable historians consider this story more legend than reality. Caesar wanted to make contact with Cleopatra and was as anxious to visit her as she was to visit him. Never considered a beauty, Cleopatra was purported to have had her charms. She was very bright and easily seduced the fifty-two-year-old Caesar. Nine months later, Cleopatra bore him a son, whom she named Caesarion. Unfortunately, Caesar never acknowledged his paternity.

With Caesar on her side, she easily defeated her younger brother, who drowned in a battle in the Nile. Caesar backed Cleopatra and arranged for her to marry her other brother, Ptolemy XIV, who was later mysteriously poisoned and died. Cleopatra then made Caesarion her coregent and successor.

Cleopatra spent a year living in Rome in one of Caesar's country houses. This did not meet with the approval of the rest of the Romans. Caesar was married, and his wife, Cornelia, was well liked. The Roman orator and statesman Cicero was particularly critical and considered Cleopatra nothing but a whore. His assessment did a lot to discredit her reputation. When Caesar was murdered in the senate, Cleopatra made a hasty retreat back to Alexandria.

There were several contenders for Caesar's position, but Mark Anthony triumphed. A complicated man who was at his best in a war setting, Anthony was attracted to Cleopatra for her wealth. Cleopatra, in kind, needed Anthony, with his legions of soldiers, to help her maintain her realm.

When Anthony was in Tarsus, a seaport on the coast of what is now Turkey, he summoned Cleopatra. She was only too happy to comply. With a flair for the dramatic, Cleopatra arrived on a barge with purple silk sails and silver oarlocks. She invited Anthony to dine on her barge. He readily succumbed to her charms.

In 41 BC, Cleopatra succeeded in having Anthony kill her sister, Artemis, who was staying at a temple in Ephesus. Much to the horror of the Romans, the execution was carried out on the steps of the temple.

Cleopatra and Anthony quickly formed a relationship. On December 25, 40 BC, Cleopatra presented Anthony with twins, Alexander Helios and Cleopatra Selene II. Anthony returned to Rome, and they were apart for four years. When Anthony returned to Egypt, he lived in Alexandria with Cleopatra. The two were married under Egyptian law, despite the fact that he was married in Rome to Octavia, the sister of Octavian, his fellow triumvir. Cleopatra and Anthony had another son, Ptolemy Philadelphus.

Cleopatra is said to have showered Anthony with material gifts. At one sumptuous dinner party, she gave him all the gold dinner plates. She then removed her string of pearls and placed them into a cup of wine. The pearls were purported to have dissolved, and she then drank the mixture. Later tests have suggested that the solution was vinegar, not wine, but the effect must have been spectacular.

The end of Cleopatra and Anthony's life was not a happy one. Anthony was summoned to Greece to fight Octavian, the titular head of Rome and his brother-in-law. Once there, he tried to divorce his wife, Octavia, who was greatly loved as a virtuous and wealthy woman in her own right. The battle did not go well. Anthony asked Cleopatra for reinforcements. When she arrived and saw that the conflict was going badly, she retreated to Egypt. Anthony followed her, believing she had betrayed him.

Cleopatra was terrified of Octavian. She filled her mausoleum with treasure. When she heard that Anthony had followed her to Egypt, she called to him. He had been so distraught that he had attempted to kill himself. His efforts were unsuccessful. However, he died shortly after his servants brought him to Cleopatra.

Octavian was terrified that Cleopatra would destroy her fortune and kill herself. When he invaded Alexandria, he was delighted to find her intact, along with her treasure. He posted guards outside her bedroom door and allowed only her two handmaidens to accompany her. The exact details of the end of her life are murky. The popular version is that she called for a basket of figs. When it was brought to her, it had an asp (a type of snake) concealed in the bottom. The asp is said to have killed her and her two servants. Some scientists say an asp would not have had enough venom to kill three women and that Cleopatra, who regularly experimented with poisons, drank a combination of hemlock and opium.

News of her death was so well received in Rome that interest rates dropped from 12 percent to 4 percent. Caesarion, Cleopatra's son with Caesar, and Octavian were proclaimed pharaohs of Egypt. However, Caesarion was killed in battle shortly after his rise to the throne, ending the rule of the pharaohs.

Our good friends, Diane and Jim, approached us and asked if they could give a theme party. It was a very generous gesture. Diane and I shared the cooking.

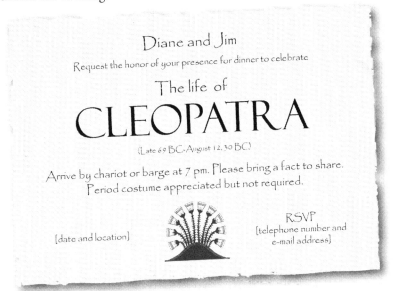

Diane and Jim

Request the honor of your presence for dinner to celebrate

The life of

CLEOPATRA

(Late 69 BC–August 12, 30 BC)

Arrive by chariot or barge at 7 pm. Please bring a fact to share.
Period costume appreciated but not required.

[date and location]

RSVP
[telephone number and
e-mail address]

Table Setting

Sam and I had been to Egypt earlier that year, where I had gotten a large, cream-colored tablecloth with twelve matching napkins. The cloth had red, green, and yellow motifs of Egyptian life and hieroglyphics, much like the images we saw inside the pyramids. The Egyptians are famous for their cotton, and it is still a great place to acquire linens. It seemed only fitting to give it to Diane for her table; she put her own glorious touch on the finished table. Read the Postmortem section for full details.

One of the other guests, Pauline Runkle, is a famous floral designer. Diane invited her to do the arrangement for the center of the table. In the spirit of Cleopatra entertaining Mark Anthony for the first time, Pauline arranged a breathtaking bouquet of roses. She then explained that Cleopatra laid a trail of roses leading Mark Anthony to his first audience with her in Tarsus.

Music

Finding appropriate music for this party was difficult. A search on the Internet was less than satisfactory. However, I did find a British rhythm-and-blues band named Cleopatra, which had a hit album in the late 1990s. It comprised three sisters: Cleo, Yonah, and Zainam Higgins. Their albums featured colorful pictures of Cleopatra in her finest regalia.

You could throw historical accuracy off the barge and play the soundtrack of *Joseph and the Amazing Technicolor Dreamcoat*, a Middle Eastern musical based on Christian biblical times. Andrew Lloyd Webber's score is infectious and certainly puts everyone in a lively party mood.

Menu for Twelve

Hors d'oeuvres
Baba Ghanoush (Eggplant Dip)
Hummus with Celery, Carrots, and Olives
Dates Filled with Goat Cheese

First Course
Lentil Soup

Main Course
Shrimp and Rice
Tabbouleh
Flatbread

Dessert
Basbousa Cake
Om Aly (Mother of Aly Dessert)

Recipes

Baba Ghanoush (Eggplant Dip)
Preparation time: 1 hour and 20 minutes

3 tablespoons olive oil
5 large eggplants
4 cups chopped onions
3 cloves garlic
1 teaspoon sea salt
1 teaspoon cayenne pepper
3 tablespoons tahini paste
5 tablespoons lemon juice
Pita bread or sliced vegetables for accompaniment

Preheat the oven to 400 degrees. Rub a large, shallow baking dish with a little olive oil, and place the eggplants in it. Prick holes in the eggplants, and roast for one hour. While the eggplants are roasting, gently sauté the onions and garlic until soft. Allow the eggplants to cool, and then remove the pulp. Discard the skin, and place the pulp, onion, and garlic into a food processor; pulse until smooth, but do not overdo it. Add the salt, cayenne pepper, tahini, and lemon juice. Serve in a shallow dish with pita or sliced fresh vegetables.

Chef's Note: In the spirit of full disclosure, lemons did not arrive in Europe and the Middle East until the first century AD. They originated in Southeast Asia and were introduced first to Italy by traders. It is totally optional to eliminate the lemons if you wish to be historically accurate. However, this little bit of trivia might be fun to share with your guests. Baba ghanoush is served all over the Mediterranean in different forms. The Egyptians are famous for adding tahini to their eggplant dip.

Hummus
Preparation time: 25 minutes

1 13-ounce can chickpeas
½ cup olive oil
½ cup lemon juice
3 cloves garlic
½ cup tahini paste
½ teaspoon cumin
1 teaspoon sea salt
1 teaspoon pepper

1 tablespoon chopped parsley for garnish
Pita bread or cut raw vegetables for serving

Wash the chickpeas and place in a food processor. Add the olive oil, lemon juice, garlic, tahini paste, and cumin. Add the salt and white pepper to your liking. Serve in a shallow bowl, and garnish with parsley.

Chef's Note: Hummus has become very popular and is now readily available in the supermarket, but it is fun to try making your own. If there is any left over, you can always freeze the hummus or throw a little into a homemade soup.

Dates Filled with Goat Cheese
Preparation time: 20 minutes

12 dates
8 ounces goat cheese

Chill the dates for about ten minutes. Remove from the refrigerator, and split each date in two. Remove the seed. Gently fill the cavity with goat cheese.

Chef's Note: You can make these up in the morning; wrap them tightly and serve at room temperature. The dates and goat cheese keep remarkably well. Dates are among the oldest foods on the planet and are native to the Middle East. Botanists think they were here five thousand years ago.

Lentil Soup
Preparation time: 25 minutes

1 pound dried lentils
10 cups chicken or beef stock
3 cups medium onions
1 cup celery
2½ cups carrots
5 cloves garlic
2 teaspoons cumin
Salt and pepper
2 tablespoons lemon juice

Cover the dried lentils with water, and soak overnight. Drain the beans, and discard the water. Place the stock and lentils in a large pot. Bring to a boil, lower the temperature to simmer, and cover. Simmer beans for one hour. Chop the onions, celery, garlic, and carrots. Add to the lentils, cover again, and simmer for another twenty-five minutes. Add the cumin, salt, pepper, and lemon juice to your liking. Make this a day or two ahead of time. Reheat and serve. The Egyptians always serve soups hot even in the blistering desert heat!

Chef's Note: This soup freezes beautifully if there is any left over. You can also serve it with a little yogurt on top.

Shrimp and Rice
Preparation time: 45 minutes (Best made a day ahead.)

2 tablespoons olive or peanut oil
3 pounds shrimp (25–30 count), with shells removed
2 cups onions
5 cloves garlic
1 tablespoon cumin
Salt and pepper
1 tablespoon cardamom
4 red chilies
5 cups rice
6 cups chicken stock

Heat one tablespoon olive or peanut oil in a pan, and fry the shrimp, onions, and garlic. Stir until the shrimp turn pink. Add the other tablespoon of oil along with the cumin, salt, pepper, cardamom, and chili to the shrimp. Stir until well blended. Add the rice and stock. Bring to a boil, and reduce the heat. Simmer for about twenty-five minutes, until the rice has absorbed the stock. Place into an ovenproof casserole dish. Reheat at 325 degrees for half an hour.

Chef's Note: This dish is truly delicious. Make a day ahead of time. Chances are you will not have any leftovers.

Tabbouleh
Preparation time: 1 hour

1½ cups bulgur
3 cups boiling water
½ to ¾ cup olive oil
5 cups Italian parsley
3 lemons
Salt and pepper
8 red cherry tomatoes
Pita bread for accompaniment

Place the bulgur in a large bowl, and cover with boiling water. Let the mixture sit for thirty minutes, or until the water is absorbed. Then add the olive oil, and let it rest for another ten minutes. Wash and clean the parsley; remove the stems and chop finely. Add to the bulgur mixture. Squeeze the lemons, and add the juice to the salad along with salt and pepper. Place the tabbouleh on a shallow large dish. Cut the cherry tomatoes in half, and place in a ring around the tabbouleh. Serve in a shallow dish with pita bread.

Chef's Note: The Egyptians cultivated wheat during Cleopatra's time. This dish is extremely healthy. Tabbouleh is best made the day before your party. This is one of those dishes that you can feel comfortable improvising on a bit. Not all bulgur is the same, and the amount of lemon juice from each lemon is a variable. Feel free to mix and taste. I once had a Lebanese neighbor who taught me how to make this wonderful dish. She would always insist there should be no "white of the bulgur" showing.

Basbousa Cake
Preparation time: 20 minutes

½ cup sugar
1 cup coconut flakes
1 teaspoon double-acting baking powder
2 cups semolina
1 cup clarified butter
1 cup milk
1 teaspoon yogurt
1 cup slivered almonds

Preheat the oven to 350 degrees, and butter a nine-inch springform pan. Mix the sugar, coconut, baking powder, and semolina together in a bowl, and set aside. Place the milk and butter in a pan, and bring to a boil. Remove the pan from the stove, and add the semolina mixture. Add the almonds and yogurt. Bake for twenty-five to thirty minutes. Run a small knife into the cake. If it comes out clean, the cake is done. Do not overbake.

Basbousa Cake Syrup

1 cup water
3/4 cup sugar
1/4 cup lemon juice

To prepare the syrup, place the sugar and water in a saucepan and bring to a boil. Lower the heat, and simmer uncovered for ten minutes. Add the lemon juice. Allow to cool. Remove the cake from the pan, and slowly drizzle the syrup over it. It will take several applications for the cake to absorb all the syrup. Feel free to let the cake sit for ten or fifteen minutes, and add more syrup.

Chef's Note: Ovens vary even in professional kitchens, so trust your instincts and check the cake for doneness. You will get to know your own oven.

Om Aly (Mother of Aly Dessert)
Preparation time: 1½ hours

1 cup white raisins
1-pound package frozen puff pastry
1 tablespoon butter
2 cups roasted almonds, hazelnuts, and pistachio nuts
2 cups milk
1 cup whipping cream
12 tablespoons brown sugar
1 teaspoon vanilla

Preheat the oven to 375 degrees. Soak the raisins in hot water for thirty minutes, and drain. While they are soaking, brush the puff pastry with butter, and bake on long cookie sheets for about twenty minutes until brown. Reduce the oven temperature to 350 degrees. Remove the pastry from the cookie sheet when it is cool enough to handle. Butter a shallow, oblong, twelve-inch baking dish. Break the pastry into two-inch to three-inch squares. Place a layer of the pastry on the bottom and then add the nuts and raisins, alternating layers. Reserve a tablespoon or two of the nut-raisin mixture for garnish. Heat the milk, cream, and vanilla with the sugar. Pour the hot milk mixture over the layers in the dish. Bake for forty minutes. Sprinkle with the remaining nuts, and serve warm.

Chef's Note: Make this the day before the party. Wrap and refrigerate. Bring to room temperature and warm slightly before serving.

Postmortem
When my good friend Diane and her supportive husband, Jim, offered to give a theme party, we bounced around a couple of names and decided on Cleopatra. I was looking for another strong female character for a theme party. We had just returned from Egypt and had bought *galabias*—long Egyptian robes—so our costumes were in place. Cleopatra's

exact birth date seems unclear, but since she died in August, we chose her for that month's event.

Diane teaches creative writing and ethics at Boston University. She invited several of her friends who were intellectually attuned to this project. Having guests relate to a subject is not always a given, but it worked beautifully this time.

Diane is a trim blond lady in excellent condition. In fact, she is probably the size of Cleopatra, who was purported to have been petite. Diane greeted us at the door in a white, diaphanous tunic that came to her thigh. The bodice was tightly tailored and wrapped with gold ribbon. She wore a black wig and an Egyptian headdress wrapped in gold. Jim wore a galabia with a gold band around his head.

The table was set opulently. Diane had borrowed my Egyptian tablecloth and placed it onto a large, circular table with a rich, red brocade cloth underneath. The goblets were deep ruby red, with matching red bowls for the soup. Underneath the bowls were gold doilies.

Pauline Runkle, our floral arranger, designed the beautiful arrangement of roses with grapes and sage. Not only was it beautiful, but it also gave off a very pleasant scent. Saucy lady that she was, Cleopatra understood sensuality. Although Cleopatra was never considered a beauty, she traded on other charms to appeal to men. Pauline told us that Cleopatra created a poultice of roses that she always wore under her clothing when she was with Mark Anthony, so that he would associate the smell of roses with her.

Roman women were not afforded anywhere near the freedoms granted Egyptian women. We exchanged many interesting facts about Cleopatra, not the least of which was her ability to eliminate her two brothers and manipulate events to her advantage.

Diane had found some beautiful poems written by Egyptian women. Each guest read one. Many were sexual, and I have since read that the ancient scripts referenced sexual intercourse freely. Several guests had read *Cleopatra: A Life*, by Stacy Schiff, which received excellent reviews. I found a marvelous book called *Cleopatra: The Last Queen of Egypt*, by Joyce Tyldesley, an English professor, which I enjoyed very much. It was enlightening to find out that Egyptian women enjoyed a measure of personal freedom and expression in their early history.

CHAPTER 10

September Dinner to Celebrate the Life of

Confucius, Chinese Philosopher

"Do not do to others what you do not want done to yourself."
-Confucius, 551 BC-479 BC

Confucius was an ancient philosopher whose life and ideas have long outlived him. He was devoted to the principle of honoring his ancestors and believed strongly that each individual should have the highest of moral standards. He was a politician, editor, teacher, and philosopher.

Confucius wanted leaders to be superior examples of moral character and inspire their subjects. (How we hunger for such high-minded leaders today.) This philosophy began in the home, where people

learnt to revere their ancestors first and then their fathers and mothers, in that order. Wives were to revere their husbands, and children were to revere their parents. This structure was a model for government. Ultimately, the teachings of Confucius evolved into a religion called Confucianism. He lived during a period in China called the Hundred Schools of Thought era.

Confucius wrote five major books that were compiled in a canon called *The Five Classics*. It presented his ideas, which he taught to seventy-five disciples. Some scholars think that some of this writing may have been amended by the interpretations of his disciples. A large body of his aphorisms was compiled after his death into a book called *The Analects*.

Confucius was born in northeastern China, in the state of Lu, in the town of Zou. His father was in the military but died when Confucius was only three years old. His mother raised him in very humble circumstances until he was old enough to work.

Confucius was married at nineteen and had a son a year later. He worked in a variety of different jobs during a turbulent time in the Lu state, where three powerful families were competing for power. However, by 501 BC, Confucius was appointed to a government position and eventually became minister of crime. Because he held no military power, he had to rely on diplomacy to achieve his goals.

It was not until his retirement from political life that Confucius really devoted himself to his philosophy. Confucius felt he had a direct link to a higher power and that he was simply the transmitter of divine teachings. One of his aphorisms is, "Heaven sends down its good or evil symbols, and wise men act accordingly." Confucius encouraged his disciples, and people in general, to closely examine situations before acting.

The Kongs, Confucius's family, can trace their ancestry back eighty-three generations. It is the oldest known family pedigree in the world. Confucius has more than two million known descendants.

Claire Cabot Taitai and Samuel Cabot Xiansheng

Humbly request your presence for a dinner to celebrate the life and teachings of

CONFUCIUS

(551 BC–479 BC)

Please bring a fact to share about Confucius

[date and location]

RSVP [telephone number and e-mail address]

Table Setting

From my research, I gathered that the Chinese do not use table settings the way we do in the West. There is to be a white tablecloth and the dishes are placed on the table, the idea being that nothing should compete with the beauty of the food being served. It was quite easy to find chopsticks, which I placed to the right of our Western cutlery. Depending on the expertise of your dinner guests, you could eliminate Western cutlery altogether.

In proper Chinese style, there should be a dish for each person. Thus, if you have eight dinner guests, you would prepare eight dishes to be shared by the entire party. After cooking five dishes, I was sufficiently exhausted to feel I had more than enough food; this was irrespective of using every dish in the kitchen.

Chinese and Western cookbooks are organized differently from one another. In the former, the chapters are arranged according to the number of guests. Thus, there is a section of dishes and menus for serving a party of four people and a section for six to eight dinner guests, with a corresponding number of dishes. Anything beyond eight guests seemed to be considered a banquet.

Music

My beloved Sam is quite the techie! He was able to download some Chinese music from the Internet on his iPhone and play it through dinner. The melodies are very soothing. In much of the music, only one instrument is played at a time.

Menu for Eight

Hors d'oeuvres
Meatballs with Chili Sauce

First Course
Egg Drop Soup

Main Course
Shrimp and Cucumbers
White Rice
Szechuan Pork
Short Ribs
Red-Cabbage Salad or Asparagus Salad

Dessert
Almond Custard with Fruit or Green-Tea Ice Cream

These dishes have been adapted to Western food preparation methods. Chinese cuisine requires a very hot fire and dishes that are prepared and eaten immediately upon creation. I must confess, I did make up these dishes earlier in the day; otherwise, I would never have had the opportunity to visit with our guests.

Recipes

Meatballs

Preparation time: 25 minutes

Dipping Sauce
4 tablespoons brown sugar
6 tablespoons soy sauce
½ cup rice vinegar
1 cup ketchup

Mix the sugar, soy sauce, rice vinegar, and ketchup together. When ready to serve, place the dipping sauce in a bowl in the center of the plate. Stick each meatball with a toothpick for easy eating, and instruct your guests to dip each meatball into the sauce.

Chef's Note: Definitely make this sauce a day ahead of time.

Meatballs
2 pounds ground chuck
2 beaten eggs
1 teaspoon salt
Dash of pepper
¼ teaspoon minced fresh garlic
½ cup bread crumbs
4 tablespoons chopped onion
1¾ cup beef stock or consommé

Mix the chuck, eggs, salt, pepper, garlic, bread crumbs, and onions together. Form the mixture into walnut-size balls. Place the stock in the top of a double boiler, and add the meatballs a few at a time. Cook for twenty-five to thirty minutes. Keep warm until ready to serve.

Chef's Note: You can make the uncooked meatballs the day before and store them, carefully wrapped, in the refrigerator. If you do so, allow them to come to room temperature before cooking.

Egg Drop Soup
Preparation time: 10 minutes

10 cups chicken stock
2 tablespoons sesame oil
¼ teaspoon sugar
2 eggs, well beaten
3 scallions, finely chopped

Boil the chicken stock in a large pot; add the sesame oil and sugar. Beat the eggs, and add to the boiling stock; remove from the heat immediately. Add the chopped scallions, and serve at once.

Chef's Note: The quality of the chicken stock is all-important. I could never figure out why Chinese chicken soups taste different from Western versions. No amount of reading can compare with interviewing an expert. A sweet Taiwanese family has a takeout restaurant near us. When I asked the woman behind the counter about their chicken stock, she explained that they put a little sesame oil and sugar in the soup. The subtle difference in flavor is remarkable. And making your own chicken stock is really worth the effort. I usually buy two roast chickens from the supermarket, remove the chicken from the bones, and place the bones in a large kettle. Cover the bones generously with water. Bring the pot to a boil, lower the temperature, and cook uncovered for four or five hours, until the flavor of the broth is strong. Strain the broth, remove the bones, and place the broth in a bowl. Cool and refrigerate. A layer of fat will form on top; remove the fat and discard. Heat and pour through cheesecloth until the broth is clear. This stock can be made well ahead of your dinner party and frozen until needed.

Shrimp and Cucumbers
Preparation time: 20 minutes

2 pounds (26 to 30 count) shrimp, peeled and deveined
4 medium-size cucumbers
2 tablespoons dry sherry
2½ tablespoons cornstarch
2 teaspoons sugar
2 teaspoons soy sauce
3 tablespoons peanut oil

Rinse and cut the shrimp into bite-size pieces. Dry on paper towels. Peel and cut the cucumbers lengthwise. Remove the seeds, and chop into small pieces. Mix the shrimp, sherry, cornstarch, and sugar together; let the mixture rest for ten minutes. Place two frying pans on the stove. Add one and a half tablespoons of peanut oil to one pan, and quickly cook the cucumbers over medium-high heat. Stir constantly until the cucumbers are translucent. Remove the pan from the heat. Add the remainder of the oil to the second frying pan, and cook the shrimp mixture over medium-high heat until the shrimp turn pink. Add the cucumbers and stir for another couple of minutes.

Chef's Note: In proper Chinese cooking, a chef would create this dish immediately before serving. However, there is no point in having people over for dinner if you cannot visit with them. I made this dish ahead of time and warmed it in a 250-degree oven before serving. Everyone ate it with gusto. You may want to add a pinch of salt. Personally, I feel the soy sauce is salty enough.

Short Ribs

Preparation time: 3 hours

3 pounds beef short ribs
2 teaspoons salt
Ground pepper
2 cloves garlic
1 tablespoon cornstarch
2 tablespoons sherry
2½ tablespoons soy sauce
2 teaspoons salt
2 tablespoons sesame oil
2 cups water
½ cup chopped scallions (optional)

Preheat the oven to 250 degrees. Place the short ribs in a shallow dish, sprinkle with salt and pepper, and cover. Roast for several hours, until the meat on the ribs is totally cooked. Set aside until cool enough to handle. Remove the meat from the bones, and slice into small pieces. Clean and chop the garlic. Combine cornstarch, sherry, soy sauce, and water. Sauté the garlic in a frying pan with sesame oil over medium heat for several minutes; add the cornstarch mixture, and stir vigorously until the sauce thickens. Add the meat, and cook for several more minutes to blend the flavors. Place in an ovenproof dish, and keep warm in a 250-degree oven until ready to serve. Just before serving, add the scallions.

Chef's Note: Most recipes call for leaving the bone in, but I like to remove it to make eating easier. In the interest of full disclosure, I took it upon myself to add the scallions. In the spirit of creating visually appealing dishes, it seemed appropriate to enhance the dark-brown dish with a bit of green.

Szechuan Pork
Preparation time: 45 minutes

3 pounds pork tenderloin
⅓ cup peanut oil
1 cup leeks
1 8-ounce can bamboo shoots
1 cup red peppers
½ cup green peppers
4 cloves garlic
4 slices ginger root
1 5-ounce can water chestnuts
⅓ cup hoisin sauce
1 cup broccoli
2 teaspoons sugar

Preheat the oven to 350 degrees. Roast the pork for twenty-five minutes. While the pork is cooking, wash the vegetables and remove the seeds from the peppers. Slice the leeks and peppers on the diagonal. Remove the outer skin of the ginger root, and slice off four pieces. Remove the tough stems from the broccoli, and cut into bite-size pieces. Drain the liquid from the water chestnuts and bamboo shoots, and cut into small pieces. Dry the vegetables. Let the pork rest for five minutes after removing from the oven. With a sharp knife, slice the pork and cut into small pieces. Heat the oil over medium to high heat. Cook the garlic and ginger first, stirring constantly. Then add the vegetables. Add the pork, and cook for another couple of minutes. Add the hoisin sauce and sugar. Make sure all the ingredients are coated in sauce. Serve immediately, or place in an ovenproof dish, cover, and keep warm in a 250-degree oven until ready to serve.

Chef's Note: You will have much better luck cooking the vegetables if they are all dry.

White Rice
Preparation time: 30 minutes

2 cups short-grain rice
6 cups water

Place the water and rice together in a pot, and bring to a rolling boil. Stir, cover, and cook for twenty minutes. Remove the rice immediately from the heat, keep covered, and let it continue to absorb the water for another ten minutes.

Chef's Note: Rice originated in China in the Pearl River valley thirteen thousand years ago. Choose rice in the Asian section of the supermarket for this meal. Follow the cooking instructions on the package.

Red-Cabbage Salad

Preparation time: 15 minutes (Prepare the day ahead.)

2 pounds red cabbage
4 tablespoons peanut oil
1 clove garlic, minced
4 tablespoons soy sauce
4 tablespoons white wine vinegar
2 tablespoons brown sugar

Remove the tough, inner white core of the cabbage and discard. Chop the heads into small pieces. Heat two tablespoons of oil in a frying pan, and cook the garlic. Add the cabbage, and stir-fry over medium-high heat until limp but not overcooked. Make sure the oil fully coats the cabbage. Remove from pan, and place in a bowl. Add the remaining ingredients to the pan, and cook for several minutes, until the brown sugar dissolves. Pour mixture over the cabbage, and toss. Place in an attractive bowl, ready to bring to the table, and refrigerate overnight.

Chef's Note: This cold dish is a nice complement to the cooked dishes on the table.

Asparagus Salad

Preparation time: 10 minutes

2 bunches fresh asparagus
4 tablespoons soy sauce
4 teaspoons sesame oil
1 teaspoon sugar
2 teaspoons minced, preserved, red ginger

Wash the asparagus, and cut the ends off on the diagonal. Place the asparagus in a frying pan, and cover with water. Cook for about six minutes, until tender. Do not overcook. While the asparagus is cooking, combine the soy sauce, sesame oil, and sugar in a bowl. Remove the asparagus, and plunge into cold water. Place it in a long, shallow dish, and cover with the dressing. Top the dish with the ginger.

Chef's Note: This dish can be made successfully the morning of the party. Refrigerate, and then allow the dish to come to room temperature before serving.

Almond Custard with Fruit
Preparation time: 15 minutes (Let set overnight.)

Custard
1 envelope unflavored gelatin
3 tablespoons sugar
8 ounces of evaporated milk
1¼ cups of water

Dissolve the gelatin in three tablespoons of water. When the gelatin is completely absorbed, it will form a thick paste; set aside. Combine the remaining water with three tablespoons of sugar, and heat until the sugar dissolves. Add the milk; do not allow it to boil. Add the gelatin mixture, and stir into the milk and sugar until well blended. Place the mixture in a square ceramic dish, and refrigerate overnight.

Fruit Syrup
1 8-ounce can mandarin oranges
5 tablespoons sugar
2 cups water
½ cup seedless green grapes
8 maraschino cherries
1 tablespoon almond extract

Drain the mandarin oranges but reserve the liquid. Dissolve the sugar in two cups of water, and add the reserved liquid from the oranges. Boil down the sauce for five to seven minutes, until it begins to thicken. Then add the grapes, oranges, and cherries. Cook for an additional five minutes, and finish by adding the almond extract. To serve, cut the custard into squares, and place in individual dessert dishes. Cover with the syrup.

Green-Tea Ice Cream
Preparation time: 40 minutes (Cure overnight.)

3 green tea bags
1 cup hot water
1 cup chopped fresh mint
2 cups half-and-half
1 cup milk
¼ teaspoon lavender extract

Brew a strong cup of green tea using three tea bags. Allow the tea to brew for five minutes. Wash the mint leaves, remove the stems, and chop. Add the mint to the tea; let sit for another five minutes. Press the mint and the tea bags in a strainer, retaining the liquid. Blend the sugar with the half-and-half and milk, until the sugar dissolves. Place the mixture in an ice-cream maker, and follow the instructions for your model. When the mixture is close to forming, add the lavender extract. Place in a container, and freeze overnight before serving.

Chef's Note: This is very much my own creation. When I had dinner at a Taiwanese restaurant with friends, we were all intrigued by the green-tea ice cream. The color of the ice cream was green, but the flavor was lacking. One of my friends suggested adding some fresh mint leaves. Her instincts were very good, indeed. I experimented with several approaches to make my own green-tea ice cream and came up with this recipe. I have refrained from adding green food coloring, but one could easily do so.

Postmortem

It is unusual to go into the house of someone who grew up on the coast of New England without seeing some Chinese memorabilia. Our region is so connected to the sea, and many fortunes were made during the China trade. Similarly, I have a great love of Chinese clothes and like to wear colorful blouses in this style. This group of *Cooking Through History* participants enjoyed dressing up in Chinese garb.

One guest, however, announced that he did not have a Chinese shirt, so he proudly sported a beautiful tie with pictures of kites. He explained that silk came from China and that the Chinese invented kites.

This dinner was a gigantic learning experience for Sam and me. I can honestly say I was so worried about the dinner that I contemplated bringing in some Chinese takeout as backup. The dishes I made were adjusted to accommodate the American palate.

The one dish I really did leave to the last minute was the egg drop soup. One of my dear friends accompanied me into the kitchen and read the instructions. She frantically whipped the eggs, while I stirred the boiling broth. The results were very successful. I served the soup in the living room in small Chinese soup bowls that could be easily raised to the mouth. After the soup, everyone came into the dining room and sat down at the table, where I had placed all six dishes in the center. I alternated the serving spoons so that three spoons faced one side of the table and three faced the other.

Sam and I were both impressed with the interactions of all our guests. There were no visual obstructions—no candlesticks or flower arrangements in the center of the table. One person spoke at a time, and everyone listened; there were not two or three conversations at once, as so often happens in Western culture. Perhaps that is more of a testament to our lovely group of "good listening" friends, but the lack of physical impediments seemed to make a difference.

Everyone had really done their research. One friend brought a lovely, woven reed basket filled with items which, he explained, could easily have been left at the grave site of Confucius. In the center of the basket was an Easter lily, a plant that originated in Asia. Surrounding the plant were small, perfectly formed, brilliant orange kumquats. They are the only citrus fruit edible with the skin and are a great delicacy in China, with many different uses. Standing up behind the lily were eight exquisite sandalwood fans, which had a very pleasing scent when opened and waved in front of the face! It was a lovely offering, and I am sure Confucius would have been grateful.

What really impressed all of us was Confucius's philosophy regarding individual responsibility and high moral conduct. Confucius felt this was particularly important for leaders. One of our learned guests, who had done business in China for several years, added that until 1916 all civil servants had to read Confucius's *Analects*. Thereafter, Confucius was considered too old-school and a hindrance to the new China.

Today, however, there seems to be a resurgence of interest around the world about the teachings of Confucius. It would be nice to think that this ancient philosopher could influence societies once again into creating a kinder world for all of us.

CHAPTER 11

October Dinner to Celebrate the Life of

John Adams, Second American President

"Patience and perseverance have a magical effect before which difficulties disappear and obstacles vanish."
-John Adams, October 30, 1735 July 4, 1826

John Adams was born in Quincy (formerly Braintree), Massachusetts. His father was a farmer and local town official, and his mother, Susanna Boylston, was from a prominent Boston family. John Adams was descended from Henry Adams, one of the early Puritans, who came to America from Devonshire, England, in 1636. John's father had hoped his son would become a minister, but the young John felt that the cloth did not offer enough intellectual freedom. He set his sights on becoming a lawyer and was one of the driving forces in the American fight for independence. In 1764, he married Abigail Smith, the daughter of a Puritan minister. She was his intellectual equal and a great confidante. They had a strong marriage, and she constantly encouraged John to uphold the ideals of freedom and independence for women as well as men.

John Adams first received recognition for his superior legal acumen after the British Parliament passed the famous Stamp Act in 1756. He went to England and argued that the tax was illegal because the people had never voted for it: it was taxation without representation. The British government capitulated and revoked the act the next year. Along with other colonists, Adams's desire for an independent America was growing stronger.

In 1770, in what was known as the Boston Massacre, British troops were prosecuted for manslaughter for their attempt to quell a demonstration. This offended Adams's sense of justice, and he agreed to represent them in a court of law. At first, this move seemed to be unpopular. But the British troops were freed of any wrongdoing, and Adams's reputation for integrity grew.

As Massachusetts representative to the Continental Congress, Adams was instrumental in creating the Declaration of Independence. He insisted that Thomas Jefferson write the historic document. Adams loved to debate. In 1778, Adams went to France to obtain a treaty of alliance. But when he found that the treaty had already been signed, he returned to Massachusetts and drafted the state's first constitution. Many other states used his draft for their own states as a model. Adams then went to Holland and persuaded the Dutch Parliament to recognize America as an independent nation and obtained a loan to finance the war.

Adams was appointed the first minister to England in 1785. He returned to America in 1788. He had a reputation for being very bright, a good debater, and scrupulously honest, but his confrontational style did not lend itself to his being a diplomat.

In 1789, Adams was elected the first vice president of the United States. During that period of American history, the candidate who received the second highest number of votes became vice president. Adams was less than thrilled about his new office, but he served the Senate competently and was reelected, along with George Washington, for a second term. During these eight years, Adams wrote *Discourses of Davila*, a series of papers describing his conservative political beliefs.

In 1797, John Adams became the second president of the United States and the first president to live in the White House. These were tumultuous times in his Federalist Party. Alexander Hamilton led half of the Federalists; John Adams, the other half. The disputes had to do with the unsettled European nations, which were going through their own revolutions and issues of trade. The French, for example, captured more than three hundred American ships, and the British captured roughly the same number. America created a navy and prepared for war. However, Adams fought hard to keep the United States from entering into a major struggle. He felt that such a move would be disastrous for the fledgling country. Adams's position cost him reelection, but the country survived because of his decision.

Adams was deeply hurt by the results of this election and refused to stay in Washington to attend Jefferson's inauguration. He returned to Quincy at the age of sixty-six. His wisdom was eventually rewarded on the issue of entering into war with France. In later years, Adams took enormous pleasure from seeing his son, John Quincy Adams, elected as the sixth president of the United States.

John Adams and Thomas Jefferson had a complicated relationship. They were good friends and allies during the formation of the United States but then had a falling out in their middle years, when they competed for the presidency. Abigail Adams did a lot to encourage the two men to heal their relationship during their retirement, before their deaths. Their correspondence is rich in reflections on many aspects of early American life. Ironically, both John Adams and Thomas Jefferson died on July 4 in 1826, the fiftieth anniversary of US independence.

Handwriting of John Adams

The forward slant of John Adams's handwriting demonstrates a person who is action oriented. Adams had a first-rate mind and exhibited both cumulative and analytical skills, with excellent attention to detail. He processed information by carefully collecting all the facts and then dissecting the findings. He had the ability to work both independently and with others. This is a characteristic often seen in salespeople.

When I compare the handwriting of Washington, Adams, and Jefferson, I am impressed by the totality of their talents. They did not always agree, but they were driven by the common goal of an independent America.

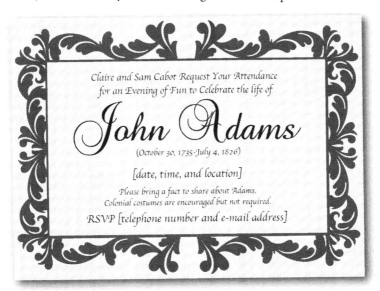

Claire and Sam Cabot Request Your Attendance
for an Evening of Fun to Celebrate the life of

John Adams

(October 30, 1735-July 4, 1826)

[date, time, and location]

Please bring a fact to share about Adams.
Colonial costumes are encouraged but not required.

RSVP [telephone number and e-mail address]

Table Setting

Most colonists loved simplicity, a sentiment that exists in Boston to this very day. New Englanders are famous for being understated. Therefore, I would suggest leaving the table without a cloth and just using place mats. If you are having the party in the summer, you might have a floral arrangement of red carnations or peonies with white candles, white linen mats, and blue napkins. You also have my permission to consider this color combination a dreadfully boring cliché! As always, take your own dining room, color schemes, and tableware into consideration.

A fall dinner party lends itself to using a pineapple as a centerpiece. A New England symbol of hospitality, pineapples were sometimes carved at the end of the meal and eaten as a treat. If a special guest was spending the evening, a gracious host might also present a pineapple to the guest to take home. Pineapples were so revered that they were frequently carved into bedposts and columns. Again, I would favor using table mats instead of a cloth for the table setting.

Music

The Public Broadcasting Service produced a marvelous series about John and Abigail Adams, which is worth borrowing from your library. In one scene, John is off at the Continental Congress and a band of patriots accompanied by a fife-and-drum corps pass the Adams farm. Abigail and her children are working in the garden but are delighted with the sound of music and stop their work.

How absolutely spectacular to find a fife-and-drum group to march up our driveway to greet our guests. As it happened, in an admission of full disclosure, we had this party in July. Some good friends from Scotland were coming for dinner. They had entertained us several times in their manor house in Cavers Carre by Melrose in Roxburghshire and had been so welcoming that we wanted to give them a memorable evening.

Sam considers me a dangerous woman with a telephone. Finding a fife-and-drum corps in our area is just the type of challenge that gets my blood flowing. I am a major fan of the National Park Service; their guides do an outstanding job. I started with a phone call to them, and one call led to another.

Eventually, I found a lovely-sounding young woman who is part of an organization called Musick of Prescott's Battalion. The group specializes in pre-1800 music and particularly relishes songs from 1775 and earlier. We worked out an arrangement where she would arrive, unbeknownst to our guests, with another fifer and a drummer. While we were having drinks outside on our porch, which is not visible from the road, they would come up the driveway playing the unmistakable tune of "Yankee Doodle Dandy." At first, the sound was faint but as they marched closer, it became louder. The three troubadours rounded the corner of the house in full colonial costumes, much to the surprised delight of our guests. They continued to play several more songs. Do make sure to read the Postmortem!

Menu for Eight

Hors d'oeuvres
Stuffed Radishes
Smoked Bluefish Pâté on Crackers

First Course
Curried Jellied Cream Consommé with Red Caviar on a
  Bed of Lettuce with Garlic Toast *or*
Clam Chowder

Main Course
Herb-Crusted Codfish
Squash Casserole or String-Beans Vinaigrette
Harvard Beets or Beets in Orange Sauce Topped with Orange Zest

Dessert
Indian Pudding or Mixed-Berry Shortcake

Recipes

Stuffed Radishes
Preparation time: 20 minutes

16 medium-size radishes
8 ounces cream cheese
¼ cup fresh herbs, such as parsley, oregano, or tarragon

Wash the radishes, and slice the bottoms so the radishes will sit flat. Carefully cut out a hollow circle in each radish with a melon ball cutter. Cream the cheese with the herbs, and fill the hollows of each radish.

Chef's Note: These can be made in the morning and refrigerated. Bring to room temperature before serving.

Smoked Bluefish Pâté
Preparation time: 25 minutes

1 smoked bluefish
⅓ cup mayonnaise
¼ cup lemon juice
¼ teaspoon horseradish
Ground pepper
Sprig of parsley for garnish
Your favorite crackers for serving

Break up the smoked bluefish in a food processor or by hand. Add the mayonnaise, lemon juice, horseradish, and ground pepper. Decorate with parsley, and serve with the crackers.

Chef's Note: Because bluefish are wild, the filets are not standard size. Use your common sense regarding the remainder of the ingredients. Begin adding the mayonnaise slowly. If your filet is large, you may need to add a little more mayonnaise and lemon juice.

Curried Jellied Cream Consommé with Red Caviar
Preparation time: 24 hours

2 tablespoons unflavored gelatin
2 10-ounce cans consommé
4 tablespoons water
1 tablespoons curry powder
12 ounces cream cheese
1 3-ounce jar red caviar
1 large head of Boston lettuce

Oil eight ramekins. Place the cream cheese and consommé in the top of a double boiler. Cover and simmer until liquefied. In the top of another double boiler, place four tablespoons of water. Sprinkle the unflavored gelatin over the water, and let absorb for at least ten minutes. Heat until the gelatin turns sticky. Add the curry powder, and stir in the cream cheese and consommé mixture until it is well blended. Divide evenly into the ramekins, and refrigerator overnight. When ready to serve, place a piece of washed lettuce on a salad plate, and unmold the jellied consommé in the center of the lettuce. Top with red caviar, and serve with garlic toast.

Garlic Toast
Preparation time: 10 minutes

2 cloves garlic

6 tablespoons butter at room temperature
8 pieces of a sliced round loaf of French bread

Set your oven on broil. Peel and mash the garlic into the butter. Place the pieces of bread under the broiler for several minutes to toast slightly. Turn over the bread, and spread the garlic butter. Run under the broiler again for another couple of minutes, until the butter mixture has melted.

Chef's Note: You can toast the first side of the bread an hour or so before your guests arrive and spread with the garlic butter. Run the bread under the broil just before serving. When planning your menu, choose either the caviar dish or the clam chowder.

Clam Chowder
Preparation time: 30 minutes

¼ pound salt pork
1 tablespoon butter
6 large yellow onions, chopped
2 quarts shucked quahogs in their juice
2 cups clam broth
2 cups cooked, diced potatoes
3 cups evaporated milk
1 cup heavy cream

Cut the salt pork into small pieces and fry. When the pork is crispy, remove from the frying pan and drain on a paper towel. Remove the fat, but do not clean the frying pan. Add the butter, and heat until melted. Add the onions, and cook until soft. Add the clams and broth, and cook for another ten minutes. Add the potatoes, milk, and cream; simmer for ten more minutes.

Chef's Note: The flavor will be better if you make the chowder the day ahead of your party.

Herb-Crusted Codfish
Preparation time: 20 minutes

¾ cup chopped parsley
¾ cup bread crumbs
4 pounds captain's cut codfish (this is a thicker cut of fish)
5 tablespoons butter

Preheat the oven to 400 degrees. Clean and wash the parsley, chop finely, and add the bread crumbs. Spread on a large plate. Wash and dry the codfish. Cut into eight good-sized pieces appropriate for serving. Melt the butter in a large frying pan, and remove from the heat. Dip the cod into the melted butter and then into the parsley mixture. Place the breaded codfish pieces in a long, shallow, buttered, ovenproof baking dish. Bake for ten to fifteen minutes. Test for doneness by sticking a fork into one of the pieces of cod. If it comes out easily, the fish is fully cooked. Serve immediately.

Chef's Note: I usually melt the butter and bread the fish an hour or so before my guests arrive. Buy the freshest codfish you can find. Do call ahead to your local fish store or supermarket and explain that you are having a dinner party and want the freshest fish available. If your fishmonger delivers, pick up the phone after your party and thank him or her. You'll probably be the only person to do so! We don't thank each other enough in this busy, overprogrammed twenty-first-century life. A few words of encouragement usually ensure good service from that day forward.

Butternut Squash Casserole
Preparation time: 1½ hours

¾ cup butter
3 cups mashed butternut squash
½ cup brown sugar
2 pounds McIntosh apples, peeled and sliced
¾ cup pecans
2 tablespoons sugar
1 tablespoon melted butter

Preheat the oven to 350 degrees. Melt half a cup of the butter, and add to the butternut squash. Add the brown sugar; reserve. In the remaining butter, fry the apple slices over medium heat for several minutes. Reduce the heat, and cook for another three minutes. Place the apples on the bottom of a casserole dish, and place the squash over the apples. For the topping, mix the pecans, sugar, and melted butter, and distribute evenly on the top of the casserole dish. Bake for twenty-five minutes.

Chef's Note: Make the casserole ahead of time up to the point of baking, refrigerate, and bring to room temperature before baking. This casserole dish is composed of two main ingredients that originated on this continent: butternut squash and pecans. Squashes were a mainstay of the Native American diet, and both Washington and Jefferson grew pecans on their estates. Pecans are the only nut indigenous to America.

Harvard Beets
Preparation time: 1 hour and 20 minutes

4 medium beets
1 tablespoon olive oil
Salt and pepper
½ cup granulated sugar
½ cup white vinegar
1½ tablespoon cornstarch
2 tablespoons unsalted butter
1 clove

Preheat the oven to 375 degrees. Scrub the beets, and cut off any tough ends. Place one beet on a piece of aluminum foil, and sprinkle with olive oil, salt, and pepper. Wrap each beet tightly, and place on a baking sheet. Cook for forty-five minutes to an hour; cool. Unwrap the beets, and peel and slice them. In the top of a double boiler, mix the vinegar, sugar, and cornstarch. After the mixture begins to thicken, add the beets, butter, and clove. Simmer for twenty minutes, until the beets are warm. Remove the clove and serve.

Chef's Note: Save yourself some time by buying very small beets so you don't have to slice them. Once again, I have adapted the recipe to twenty-first-century standards. Cornstarch was not invented until the early twentieth century; the colonists must have used flour.

John Adams was a graduate of Harvard College, established in 1636, six years after the founding of Boston. Some food historians think this dish received its name from the college's signature crimson color.

If you are celebrating your John Adams theme party in July, you might want to consider the following summer dishes.

String-Beans Vinaigrette
Preparation time: 25 minutes

24 ounces fresh string beans
1 cup sesame-oil dressing
Pinch of baking soda
2 tablespoons fresh, chopped rosemary

Wash the string beans, and cut off the ends. Place in cold water while you make the sesame-oil dressing (see recipe that follows). In a frying pan, boil enough water to cover the beans; you may have to do this in batches. Sprinkle a bit of baking soda in the water to retain the deep green of the beans. Cook the beans until tender, usually about fifteen minutes. Place the beans lengthwise in a shallow dish. Add some of the dressing (you will have plenty left over), and then add the rosemary. Serve at room temperature.

Sesame-Oil Dressing
Preparation time:

2 cloves garlic
⅓ cup olive oil
⅓ cup sesame oil
⅓ cup good-quality white balsamic vinegar
Salt and pepper

Combine all ingredients and blend well.

Chef's Note: I make this a day ahead of time and refrigerate. Allow the string beans to come to room temperature before serving. Don't hesitate to add a little more rosemary.

Beets in Orange Sauce with Orange Zest
Preparation Time: 25 minutes

6 tablespoons orange zest
4 navel oranges
8 cups canned pickled beets
1½ tablespoons butter
2 tablespoons flour
½ teaspoon salt
1 tablespoon honey
1 tablespoon lemon juice
¼ cup orange juice
4 tablespoons Cointreau

Using a handheld grater, shave the skins of the oranges until you have six level tablespoons orange zest; reserve for garnish. Cut the oranges in half, and squeeze them. Retain the juice. Next, drain the beets, and cut into bite-size pieces if they seem too big for a mouthful. Heat the butter in a frying pan. Stirring constantly, add the flour, salt, honey, lemon juice, and orange juice. Cook and stir until the sauce is smooth and well blended. Add the Cointreau last. Finally, add the beets, and coat them thoroughly with the sauce. Cool and serve at room temperature. Garnish with the orange zest.

Chef's Note: Beets, string beans, and pumpkins would have been planted by the Adams family in their garden. Root vegetables were of particular interest to colonial farmers, because they could be preserved in a root cellar during the winter.

Indian Pudding
Preparation time: 1 hour, 25 minutes

6 cups heavy cream
½ cup cornmeal
3 tablespoons butter
2 cups molasses
1½ teaspoons cinnamon
1½ teaspoons ginger
3 beaten eggs
1½ cups cold milk

Preheat the oven to 350 degrees. Butter a large, ovenproof baking dish. Scald the cream in a double boiler. Slowly add the cornmeal, and stir constantly. The cornmeal has a tendency to lump, so try to keep the stream of cornmeal flowing slowly and stir vigorously. Cook over hot water for fifteen minutes, and then add the butter, molasses, cinnamon, ginger, and eggs. Pour the mixture into the buttered dish, and cover with the cold milk. Bake for one hour, and serve warm. If making ahead of time, refrigerate. Bring the pudding to room temperature, and warm in the oven before serving.

Chef's Note: I always make Indian pudding ahead of time. After you have cooked your codfish, turn off the oven and warm the Indian pudding. Give the pudding a good stir before you serve it. It is not the best-looking dessert, but it is delicious! You can add a little vanilla ice cream if you wish.

This is a very old New England dessert. During the seventeenth century, cornmeal was called Indian meal. Corn is a New World grain. Molasses was plentiful as a result of the Boston rum trade. Traditionally, Indian pudding was cooked in a long, slow oven. However, this modern-day version is easier.

Mixed-Berry Shortcake
Preparation time: 15 minutes

Shortcake
2½ cups flour
4 tablespoons sugar

1 teaspoon ginger
2 tablespoons double-acting baking powder
1 cup unsalted butter
1½ cups buttermilk

Preheat the oven to 400 degrees, and butter a flat cooking pan. In a large bowl, mix the flour, sugar, ginger, and baking powder. Cut the butter into pieces. Combine ingredients, either by cutting with a pastry cutter or pulsing quickly in a food processor. Add the buttermilk and pulse again. After the mixture is well blended, divide into eight rounds of dough. Bake for eighteen minutes, until the dough turns a light golden brown.

Mixed Berries
4 cups fresh strawberries
4 cups fresh blueberries
¼ cup sugar
1 teaspoon lemon juice

Wash the fruit. Remove the stems from the strawberries and cut in half. Place the blueberries and strawberries in a large bowl, and cover with sugar and lemon juice.

Ginger Whipped Cream
3 cups heavy whipping cream
4 tablespoons sugar
1 teaspoon powdered ginger

Place the cream in a deep bowl, and beat vigorously. Add the sugar slowly. When the cream begins to thicken, add the ginger and blend. Beat the cream until it forms stiff peaks.

To Assemble
Split each shortcake biscuit in half. Put a generous serving of fruit over each piece of shortcake, and top with whipped cream.

Chef's Note: All the elements can be made a day ahead of time.

Postmortem

We had the original party in July, which was the month John Adams died, not the month he was born. Hence, I have included both summer and fall menu choices, keeping the cod—Massachusetts's most formidable fish—the constant.

In all honesty, we tried to impress our Scottish guests and give them a true flavor of the history of New England. A celebration of the life of Adams, a true patriot and favored son of Massachusetts, seemed appropriate.

Sam and I are getting a lot of mileage out of the colonial costumes we bought for Thomas Jefferson's dinner in April. Having read so much about this period in our history, and having visited John Adams's birthplace, we feel very comfortable in our colonial role.

The weather gods were with us. It was one of those lovely, balmy July evenings—not too hot but warm enough to let us celebrate the season. We had drinks outside, where our guests mingled, enjoying one another's company. The sound of the fife-and-drum corps coming up the driveway elicited a stirring moment of curiosity and delight. Our group of three musicians was clad in colonial costumes. After a dramatic drum roll, they came to a halt. Sam had written a short presentation. One of the fifers called to our Scottish friend, loud and clear, "Will you join us in our fight against the British?" Our Scottish friend is an accomplished businessperson and archer with the Queen's bodyguard in Scotland. In an act of supportive treason, he readily agreed that he would be glad to assist the rebel cause.

The fifer then proceeded to tell us more about the fife-and-drum corps in general. The combination of fife and drum first started in Switzerland. The sound is said to have resonated for as far as a mile under ideal conditions. The drums were used during battle to communicate with factions of forces on the field and stir people into battle. Truly, the sound is rousing.

In the United States, many fife-and-drum corps gained their greatest popularity after the Civil War. Veterans would congregate and play their instruments as a way of being together and trying to heal the enormous emotional devastation of their wartime experiences.

The song, "Yankee Doodle Dandy," which we associate with the American Revolutionary War, was originally an English nursery rhyme condemning England's military and political figure Oliver Cromwell as a "Nankee Doodle." The song became popular in America during the French and Indian War of 1754, when the colonists and British regulars fought alongside each other. The British were surprised that the Americans, whom they considered a ragtag, undisciplined group, liked the song. The British changed the lyrics from *Nankee* to *Yankee*, making fun of the Americans. *Doodle* referred to a fool and *dandy* to a gentleman. *Macaroni* was not a pasta but an eighteenth-century word referring to an Englishman dressed in the fancy Italian style. The corruption of these lyrics resulted in over 190 variations of the original song.

In between the main course and dessert, one of the couples produced a lovely little basket. The basket was carefully decorated with ribbons and contained ten questions about John Adams's life. Each piece of paper was scorched to make it look like an old document. As I have mentioned before, the success of these parties rests on the enthusiasm of the guests. This was a spectacular idea.

Here are the questions:

1. What was Adams's wife's name, and how many children did the couple have?
   Answer: Abigail. She had six births. The last child was stillborn.
2. How tall was John Adams?
   Answer: He was five feet seven inches.
3. What epidemic befell Braintree in 1776?
   Answer: Smallpox. The British allowed the afflicted to leave Boston and infiltrate American lines.
4. To what country was Adams named ambassador in 1777?
   Answer: France
5. What was the name of the ship Adams took to France in 1779?
   Answer: Sensible.
6. From what European country did Adams seek financial support?
   Answer: Holland.
7. From what malady did Adams suffer while in Amsterdam?
   Answer: Malaria.
8. What were the key issues to be negotiated with the British at the end of the war?
   Answer: Boundaries of the United States, rights of navigation on the Mississippi River, debts, the interests of Loyalists and American Tories, and American fishing rights on the Grand Banks of Newfoundland.
9. Who was the chief negotiator for the British at the end of the war, and what triumvirate of Americans represented the colonies?
   Answer: Richard Oswald, a Scot, and Henry Strachey on the British side; Adams, Franklin, and Jay on the American side.
10. How old was Adams when elected president of the United States?
    Answer: Fifty-seven.

In retrospect, it seems amazing to me that Sam and I had never thought of creating a list of questions for our other theme parties. However, it probably was better to have these questions come from one of our guests.

As the soft light of the candles burned low, our friend read the questions with great humor. At that moment you could not help but hope that John and Abigail would have enjoyed being with us. Looking around the table at our wonderful group of friends and my handsome husband outfitted with a white wig and black waistcoat, I felt like a true colonial patriot on that summer night in July.

CHAPTER 12

November Dinner to Celebrate the Life of

Indira Gandhi, First and Only Female Prime Minister of India

"You cannot shake hands with a clenched fist."
-Indira Gandhi,
November 19, 1917 October 31, 1984

Indira Gandhi was an exceptional human being with outstanding leadership skills. In 2001, she was voted India's greatest prime minister, and she was designated "Woman of the Millennium" in a British Broadcasting Corporation poll taken in 1999. She once said: "I don't think of myself as a woman, I think of myself as a person with a job to do." She was the third prime minister of India, the longest acting head of her country, and, to date, the only woman. Tragically, she was assassinated in 1984.

Indira was the only child of Jawaharlal Nehru, the first prime minister and founding head of the Republic of India, which received its independence in 1947 after two hundred years of rule by Great Britain. To fully understand Indira, one must fully appreciate India and its culture. It is family oriented, and these family connections were a natural path for her ascent to power.

Indira was born in Allahabad into a wealthy family. Her father had been educated in England. Indira's mother was very beautiful but often sick with tuberculosis, from which she eventually died. Indira's childhood was a lonely one, as she was taught at home by tutors. In 1934, she was sent to Viswa Bharati University in Shantiniketan. However, her mother's health was so poor that her father sent them both to England, where Indira attended Oxford. Her studies were cut short to care for her mother, who was taken to Switzerland, where she eventually died of tuberculosis.

Indira then became her father's hostess. By this time, Nehru was the prime minister and often traveled abroad. Indira charmed people. She was beautiful and very clever. Mahatma Gandhi was a close friend of Nehru, and Indira had the benefit of knowing these two great men who were not only dedicated to India but wise and clever political leaders.

Nehru died unexpectedly of a heart attack in 1964. The next prime minister, Lal Bahadur Shastri, died after eighteen months in office. By this time Indira was married and serving in the upper house of the Parliament of India. The older members of the Indian National Congress thought that by proposing Indira for prime minister they could control her. Clearly, they would be proven wrong.

Indira was once interviewed by a reporter, who said, "Many people feel you are a *gungi gudiya* (dumb doll)." She simply replied, "Well, people are all entitled to their own opinion." This clever answer gives you great insight into a born leader with enormous self-confidence.

During her first tour as prime minister, from 1966 to 1977, Indira experienced many challenges, among them the formation of East Pakistan into Bangladesh. When she was accused of election fraud in 1977, she not only lost that election but spent a brief time in jail. People felt sorry for her.

She ran again in 1980, on a platform to eradicate poverty. Indira Gandhi was beginning to be thought of as the "mother of India." Her campaign worked, and she remained in office until 1984, when she was assassinated by her two Sikh bodyguards. They killed her in retribution for sending the army into the Golden Temple, the holiest of all Sikh sites.

Handwriting of Indira Gandhi

The vertical script of Indira Gandhi indicates a reserved personality. She would have liked to have known where she was going before she acted. She always liked to work alone, despite her collection of advisors, and was often criticized for not listening to them. Her strong determination is one of her most prominent characteristics. Perhaps as a result of being an only child, her handwriting shows that she liked to keep her emotional distance from people, even those she loved.

Rani Claire Cabot and Raja Samuel Cabot

request the pleasure of your company for dinner to celebrate the life of

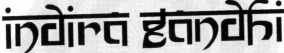

indira gandhi

(November 19, 1917–October 31, 1984)

[date, time, and location]

Please bring a fact to share with the other guests. Dhotis and saris appreciated but not required.

RSVP [telephone number and e-mail address]

Table Setting

Like many of our other theme parties, this one was prompted by our travels. If you can't go to India, you might contemplate renting a Bollywood movie. The first thing that impressed me from our journey to India was the enormous reverence the people have for color. Many of the women wore beautiful saris in a full rainbow of colors: red, green, purple, turquoise, and yellow. If you could think of a color, it was right in front of you, wrapped around a graceful woman. Therefore, I wanted my table to reflect this mood. We had bought some long table runners made from old saris. The workmanship and reverence for crafts and needlework of any type is inspiring. This runner was a great example—a freestyle pattern with a backdrop of green and extensive bead work.

Perhaps you are like me and have a hard time throwing things away. Over the years, china and glassware get broken. But in my mind, this does not diminish the beauty of the remaining pieces. They wait silently in a dark cupboard, hoping to be drafted into service, like an aging butler from *Downton Abbey*. A set of eight lovely goblets becomes seven; a set of twelve hollow, fluted champagne glasses—always used by my mother for Christmas dinner—are down to six.

In India, diversity is commonplace. There are twenty-nine states, four major religions, and ten major languages, all united by English. In this spirit, it occurred to me that it would be fun to combine these odd bits of glassware. So, I alternated goblets: four of one style for the men and four of another style for the women.

Everywhere you go in India, you see marigolds. They are strung in necklaces and often presented to you when you arrive at a hotel. So marigolds were a must on the table, along with low, small candles to draw everyone's eye to the exquisite runner, with its undulating pattern.

Music

The most widely known Indian instrument is the sitar, a stringed instrument with a very long neck. Hindu and Karnatak music use a set of pitches and small motives. I was able to find a CD called *Sounds of India*, by Ravi Shankar. If you want something a little less traditional, another CD, *Bollywood Anthology of Songs from Popular Indian Cinema*, is available from Amazon.

Menu for Eight

Hors d'oeuvres
Samosas with Major Grey's Chutney

First Course
Tandoori Shrimp on a Bed of Lettuce

Main Course
Chicken Curry
Saffron Rice
Accompanied by:
Tomato Chutney
Cashews or Peanuts
Chopped Onions
Yogurt and Cucumbers
Coconut
Sliced Bananas
Red Pepper Flakes

Dessert
Gavjar Halwa (Carrot Pudding)

Recipes

Samosas

Preparation time: 25 minutes

¼ cup bread crumbs
4 tablespoons milk
½ pound ground hamburger meat
¼ cup chopped fresh cilantro
1 beaten egg
1 teaspoon curry powder
¼ cup chopped onions
Salt and pepper
2 tablespoons vegetable oil
1 piece commercially prepared puff pastry, nine inches by five inches
2 tablespoons flour, for rolling the dough
8 ounces Major Grey's Chutney

Preheat oven to 425 degrees. Oil a large baking sheet. Moisten the bread crumbs with the milk, and let sit for ten minutes. Mix the hamburger meat, cilantro, egg, curry powder, onions, salt, and pepper together. Set aside. Spread a little flour on your counter (a marble or granite surface is perfect), and roll out the puff pastry; cut circles with a three-inch cookie cutter. Place a bit of the meat mixture on top of the pastry, and fold in half. Crimp the edges with a fork, leaving little marks on one side of the samosa. Place on the oiled cookie sheet, and bake for fifteen to twenty minutes, until browned.

Chef's Note: If you don't have a three-inch cookie cutter, don't panic. Just use a juice glass turned upside down. Remember, these are hors d'oeuvres, so you want them to be small enough to eat comfortably while standing up. Pass the samosas with Major Grey's Chutney.

Tandoori Shrimp on a Bed of Lettuce

Preparation time: 10 minutes (Marinate for three hours.)

2 pounds (26 to 30 count) shrimp, peeled and deveined
1 cup plain yogurt
2½ tablespoons tamarind paste
1 teaspoon coriander
3 tablespoons lime juice
1½ heads boston lettuce
2 tablespoons olive oil
Pinch of salt
½ lemon

Mix the yogurt, tamarind, coriander, and lime juice together. Add the shrimp, cover, and marinate in the refrigerator for at least three hours. When ready to serve, place the shrimp on a well-oiled pan, and broil them on each side for five to seven minutes, until they are pink. Toss the lettuce leaves in oil, salt, and a little lemon juice. Place a few leaves on each salad plate. Divide the cooked shrimp evenly and serve.

Chef's Note: You can easily enlarge the portions and serve the shrimp and lettuce as a summer lunch dish with rice.

Chicken Curry
Preparation time: 3 hours

4 teaspoons coriander
3 teaspoons cumin
4 teaspoons turmeric
2 teaspoons curry powder
1 teaspoon cinnamon
3 teaspoons butter or ghee
2 cloves garlic
1 cup chopped onions
2 apples, peeled and cored
2 cloves garlic
1 2-inch piece of ginger, chopped
8 hard-boiled eggs
10 cups chicken stock
16 ounces coconut milk
1½ cups chopped tomato
2 bay leaves
4 to 5 tablespoons cornstarch
4 to 5 tablespoons water
8 cups chopped, cooked chicken

This recipe is not difficult, but it is time consuming. Think of the procedure in three steps: First, prepare the spices. Then, prepare the sauce. Finally, add the chicken.

Prepare the spices first. In a small bowl, combine the coriander, cumin, turmeric, curry, and cinnamon. Place the spices in a small, frying pan (preferably nonstick), turn the heat to medium, and shake the pan back and forth for a minute so the contents do not burn; remove immediately. This maximizes the flavor of the spices. Put aside.

Then, prepare the sauce. In a large pot, melt the butter or ghee, and add the garlic, onions, apples, and ginger. Sauté over low heat until the mixture is translucent; this will probably take around five to ten minutes. Add the hard-boiled eggs, chicken stock, coconut milk, tomatoes, and bay leaves. Cook on low heat for another five minutes. Add the warmed spices, stir well, and reduce the heat to a simmer. Cover the pot, and simmer for two and a half hours. Remove about one-quarter to one-half cup of the stock, pour it into a separate bowl, and mix with the cornstarch. When the cornstarch and broth are well blended, return this mixture to the pot on the stove. Continue to stir until the sauce thickens. Stir often, being careful not to damage the hard-boiled eggs.

Last, add the diced chicken. Cook for half an hour. Remove the bay leaf before serving.

Chef's Note: I always make this dish a day or two ahead. On party day, remove the curry from the refrigerator at least forty-five minutes before cooking, and allow it to come to room temperature. You can either reheat this dish on top of the stove or place it in a casserole dish, uncovered, in a 350-degree oven for thirty-five to forty minutes.

Saffron Rice
Preparation time: 50 minutes

2 cups brown rice
5 cups water or chicken stock
1 teaspoon vegetable oil
1 teaspoon saffron

Bring water or stock to a boil. Stir in rice, saffron, and oil. Cover, and lower the heat. Cook for forty-five minutes.

Chef's Note: You can cook the rice ahead of time and place it in a strainer over hot water. This keeps it warm and moist.

Tomato Chutney
Preparation time: 1 hour and 20 minutes

3 cloves garlic
2 2½-inch pieces of fresh ginger
1½ cups red wine vinegar
1 20-ounce can tomatoes
1 cup sugar
⅛ teaspoon cayenne pepper
3 tablespoons raisins
4 sterilized, pint-size mason jars

Peel the garlic and ginger, and place in a food processor with half the vinegar. Turn to high, and blend thoroughly. Add the tomatoes and raisins to a large pot on top of the stove, and add the blended garlic and ginger mixture. Add the remaining cup of vinegar, salt, and cayenne pepper. Bring to a boil, and then simmer, uncovered, at a very low temperature for one hour. Stir often to make sure the mixture does not burn the bottom of the pan. Cool, and place into a sterilized jar. Place the jars in hot water, and cook for thirty minutes.

Chef's Note: This chutney is very good. But I also served Major Grey's Chutney, which is a mango chutney available from any good supermarket.

Yogurt and Cucumbers
Preparation Time: 15 minutes

1 cup yogurt
1 large cucumber

Peel the cucumber, and slice lengthwise into three stalks. Remove the seeds, and chop. Add a little salt, and let the mixture sit for about ten minutes. Drain the cucumbers, which will probably be quite watery. Mix with the yogurt, and serve with the curry. This refreshing dish offsets the hot spices of the curry. When ready to serve the curry and rice, place all the condiments (i.e., tomato chutney, cashews or peanuts, chopped onions, coconut, sliced bananas, and red pepper flakes) in small bowls. Place these on the table for the guests to help themselves.

Gajar Halwa (Carrot Pudding)
Preparation time: 40 minutes

2 pounds young carrots
3½ cups light cream
1 cup brown sugar
1 cup golden raisins
¼ cup melted unsalted butter
1 teaspoon allspice
½ cup chopped toasted almonds

Peel the carrots, and grate or chop very fine. Place them in a pan on top of the stove, and add the cream. Bring to a boil, cover, and reduce the heat. Simmer until the carrots are soft. Add the brown sugar, raisins, butter, and allspice. Stir well, cover, and cook on low for another fifteen minutes. The pudding will be a thick mixture. Cool and chill. Scatter almonds on a baking sheet, and set the broiler on high. Watching closely, toast the almonds for a few minutes on each side until they are a light brown. Place the pudding in individual dessert cups, and top with the chopped almonds before serving. You can also bring the pudding to the table in one large bowl and serve each guest.

Postmortem

Theme dinners are often a good time to invite an out-of-town guest. One of my good friends, Alison, came up from Old Lyme, Connecticut, where I used to live. She is one of the few people I enjoy working beside in the kitchen. It was her idea to cook the rice ahead of time and steam it. The results were very successful, indeed. She also brought the quote from Indira in the epigraph.

Sam and I had acquired some Indian clothes on our visit to India, so of course we wore them. Needless to say, we love it when guests get into the spirit of the party and come in costumes. One guest borrowed a dhoti from his Indian son-in-law, which fit him perfectly. The long off-white cotton coat had a Nehru collar and came with drawstring trousers.

Another guest had studied Mahatma Gandhi instead of Indira. People often wonder about the relationship and if Indira was related to Mahatma. She was not, but she did know Mahatma very well; he was a good friend of her father, Jawaharlal Nehru. The two men collaborated to form an independent India. Indira would have seen Mahatma often at the Nehrus' house.

Indira married a man named Feroze Gandhi in 1942. He was a politician and journalist who later became the publisher of the National Herald. They had two sons, one of whom, Rajiv Gandhi, also became a prime minister—only to be assassinated like his mother.

As is often the case, conversations take on a life of their own—not necessarily on message but related to the subject. One of our guests is a great raconteur and recited a poem by Rudyard Kipling, entitled "If." Kipling was born in Bombay, India, in 1865 and wrote many poems about his early childhood.

At the end of the evening, when we were getting ready to snuggle down for a well-deserved night's sleep, I asked Sam how he thought the evening went.

"Honestly, why on earth did you use two different types of wine glasses? It looked as if we couldn't afford a full set," he said.

"I was trying to reflect the diversity of India, revering their spiritual heritage of uniting three major religious groups and widely different geographical areas," I replied.

"Oh, I see, so that was it." Before I could really say anything else, he had fallen asleep. Sam has a remarkable talent for drifting off to dreamland within seconds of hitting the pillow.

CHAPTER 13

December Dinner to Honor the Life of

Giacomo Puccini, Italian Composer

"Inspiration is an awakening, a quickening of all man's faculties,
and it is manifested in all high artistic achievements."
~Giacomo Puccini,
December 22, 1858-November 29, 1924

Giacomo Puccini's personal life was as dramatic as the operas he wrote. The melodious tones and powerful solos of his music are infectious, even for those who profess not to like opera. I swear, his music improves my cooking and makes the ingredients happier to participate in the creation of any savory dish!

If family legacy is an inherent ingredient in success, Puccini was well positioned. He came from five generations of musicians. Giacomo was born in the ancient, walled city of Lucca in the Tuscany region of Italy. It is a magnificent city, with a deep history that dates back to the Etruscans. Music of all types can be heard as you walk down the street.

Sadly, Puccini's father died when he was only five. His mother sent him to study with his uncle Magi, the local choirmaster and organist in Lucca. Legend has it that at the age of seventeen, Puccini heard Verde's *Aida*. From that moment forward, he gave up his studies with his uncle and was determined to write operas. He was so enamored of *Aida* that he persuaded his brother, Michael, to walk eighteen and a half miles to Pisa so they could catch another performance.

At the age of twenty-one, Puccini won a scholarship to the Milan Conservatory. His principal course of study was composition. Shortly after arriving, he wrote the *Messa di Gloria*. The story chronicles his family's relationship with church music. Two years later, Puccini entered a contest for a one-act opera. He did not win, but his work was performed at Teatro Dal Verme.

Fame did not come without hard work. Puccini had difficulty working with several librettists. After the failure of his opera *Edgar*, Puccini formed a collaboration with Illica and Giacosa. Together the three produced *La Bohème*, *Tosca*, and *Madama Butterfly*. *La Bohème* was based on Puccini's student days at the Milan Conservatory. It is a great introduction to opera for any newcomer to that style of music. In fact, *La Bohème* is performed more than any other opera.

Puccini's success afforded him the ability to buy land and build a villa on Lake Massaciuccoli, in the village of Torre del Lago. Puccini is buried in the chapel on the property with his wife and son. His villa is now a museum.

Puccini's passion for women, boats, and fast cars was as predictable as his passion for music. He fell in love with Elvira, the wife of his friend. Despite her marital status, Elvira lived with Puccini. However, Puccini's constant infidelity drove Elvira mad. She continually harassed her maid, Doria, accusing her of having an affair with Puccini. Doria eventually committed suicide. The autopsy proved that Doria was a virgin, and Elvira was sent to jail for five months.

Puccini smoked cigarettes and Toscano cigars heavily. He was diagnosed with throat cancer in 1924. He died of a heart attack while receiving treatment for throat cancer in Brussels.

Puccini's finale opera was *Turandot*. He did not live to finish the score, which was completed by Franco Alfano. When Toscanini, the famous early-twentieth-century conductor, performed *Turandot* for the first time, he stopped the music where Puccini had finished it. Turning to the sold-out audience, he is purported to have said, "Here the opera finishes, because at this point the maestro died." Toscanini then picked up the baton, turned to the audience, and said, "But his disciples finished his work." It was a dramatic finale to one who understood drama so well himself. One hopes Puccini's spirit was watching from heaven.

Handwriting of Giacomo Puccini

Not surprisingly, Puccini's handwriting shows enormous passion. It also displays tremendous vision and imagination. He was dominating and probably not an easy personality to be around. Puccini had a great sense of timing. This is a characteristic common in musicians as well as athletes. He was self-reliant to the point of finding it difficult to trust others.

Signore y Signora Cabot
invite you to dinner with music
and good food to celebrate the life of

Giacomo Puccini
(December 22, 1858-November 29, 1924)

Please come and bring a fact to share about Puccini's life.
[date, time, and location]
RSVP [telephone number and email address
Dress: Black tie suggested
but not required

Table Setting

It must have been something to see people arriving to an opera performance in the early twentieth century. There was no television; entertainment, for the most part, was live. A night out was a treat, and people dressed for the occasion. The opera was not only a place to be entertained but also a place to be seen. I wanted our dining-room table to reflect the drama of an opera and the celebratory spirit of the Christmas holiday season. So, why not use a red tablecloth? Red is the color of passion and excitement! Everything about Puccini was dramatic. For those of us in New England, the warmth of the bright-red tablecloth is in direct contrast to the cold outside.

For fun, I took some branches and spray-painted them silver. These were very pretty when combined with white roses and greens in the center of the table. By chance, I came across some deep-plum-colored candles. If this combination of red and purple seems too garish for you, simply use white or silver candles. Note: If you want to spray-paint branches for your dining-room table, do so a few days or a week ahead of the party.

Music

Oh my, is there any question? To walk into a house and hear the score from *Turandot* or *La Bohème* along with the rich aroma of a good meal in the offing is like falling into a feathered bed scented with heavenly perfume! There are many renditions of Puccini's operas on CD, with and without vocals; choose your preference.

Menu for Eight

Hors d'oeuvres
Cheese-and-Salami Sticks

First Course
Tuscan Bean Soup with Italian Bread

Main Course
Osso Buco
Risotto or Baked Artichoke and Cheese Pie
Roasted Asparagus

Dessert
Olive-Oil Cake with Clementines

Recipes

Cheese-and-Salami Sticks
Preparation time: 15 minutes

¼ pound sharp cheddar cheese
¼ pound salami
1 6-ounce jar green olives with pimientos
1 large bunch fresh basil
1 box uncolored toothpicks

Cut the cheese and salami into small cubes. Wash and dry the basil. Spear a small piece of cheese, followed by a small piece of salami, a piece of basil, and an olive onto each toothpick. Arrange on a plate and pass around.

Chef's Note: You can make these up early on the day of your party. Wrap them carefully and refrigerate. Bring to room temperature before serving.

Tuscan Bean Soup
Preparation time: 35 minutes

6 cloves garlic
2 tablespoons olive oil
3 cups chopped leeks

8 cups chicken stock
1 14-ounce can cannellini beans
1 14-ounce can black beans
2 tablespoons each fresh rosemary, thyme, and parsley
Salt and pepper
¼ cup freshly grated Parmesan cheese

Place the olive oil in a large kettle. Simmer the leeks for ten to fifteen minutes, until soft. Add the chicken stock, cannellini beans, garlic, and black beans. Simmer for twenty minutes. Add the rosemary, thyme, parsley, salt, and pepper. Simmer for an additional twenty minutes. When ready to serve, pass the grated Parmesan in a bowl for guests to serve themselves.

Chef's Note: If you use dried cannellini and black beans, cover them completely with water and soak overnight. Simmer for forty minutes or so until thoroughly cooked. Drain any excess liquid and add to your soup.

Osso Buco
Preparation time: 2½ hours

Osso buco literally means "bone with a hole," which refers to the marrow inside the slice of veal. It is a Milanese dish and was originally served with gremolata, a condiment of parsley, lemon zest, and garlic. Ask your butcher for help in choosing the correct cut of meat. You may have to order ahead of time.

¼ cup olive oil
32 precut pieces of veal shank, cross cut (order from butcher)
3 large carrots
3 large chopped onions
6 cloves chopped garlic
2 6-ounce cans tomato paste
1 cup red wine
3 10-ounce cans consommé
1 bay leaf
2 tablespoons each thyme, oregano, and rosemary
Salt and pepper

Preheat the oven to 275 degrees. Put the olive oil into a large pot on the stove. Turn the heat up to medium high, and sear each piece of veal shank. Add more olive oil if needed. Place the seared meat into a large, shallow, ovenproof pan and keep warm in the oven while you make the sauce. Continue until all the pieces of meat are seared, adding more olive oil to the frying pan if needed.

Now make the sauce. In the same pan used for searing the meat, add the carrots, onions, and garlic. Turn the heat to low, cover the pot, and simmer the vegetables for about ten to fifteen minutes; stir frequently to prevent burning. Next, add the tomato paste, red wine, consommé, bay leaf, thyme, oregano, rosemary, salt, and pepper. Stir often over medium-low heat for ten more minutes, until the sauce is well blended.

Finally, pour this sauce over the veal pieces in the baking dish. Make sure each piece is well covered with sauce. Cover and place in the oven for one hour. Remove the pan and turn over the pieces of veal shank, making sure to scoop the sauce over the top of each piece. Return to the oven, cover, and cook for another hour. Serve on warm plates, and top each veal shank with a little of the gremolata sauce (see recipe that follows).

Chef's Note: I usually make this dish the day before the party. Remove from the refrigerator an hour before reheating. Preheat the oven to 325 degrees and reheat for fifteen minutes, remove the cover, and cook for fifteen minutes more. Top with gremolata sauce and serve at once.

Gremolata Sauce
Preparation time: 10 minutes

5 tablespoons finely chopped Italian parsley
3 cloves garlic, minced
2 tablespoons grated lemon zest
3 minced anchovy filets
1 teaspoon olive oil

Chop the parsley and garlic. Combine with the lemon zest, anchovies, and olive oil. Place a small amount of the sauce on top of the osso buco before serving.

Chef's Note: If you look at the ingredients of gremolata sauce, does it remind you of the ingredients for chimichurri sauce in the May event for Evita Perón? There were many Italian immigrants who went to Argentina. They brought and adapted their dishes to their new country.

Risotto
Preparation time: 25 minutes

8 cups chicken stock
3 tablespoons unsalted butter

1 medium red onion, finely chopped
2 cloves garlic
2⅓ cups arborio rice
½ cup freshly grated Pecorino Romano cheese
3 tablespoons extra virgin olive oil
Sea salt and ground pepper

Heat the chicken stock in a pot on the stove. In another large pot, melt one and a half tablespoons of butter. Add the onions and garlic. Sauté gently over low heat with a wooden spoon or spatula and add the rice, stirring constantly to coat the rice with butter. This should take two to three minutes. Begin adding the chicken stock, half a cup at a time, and continue to stir until you have used all of the stock. The rice should be firm but fully cooked, and the entire dish should look like oatmeal. Now, add the cheese, olive oil, salt, and pepper. When all of these ingredients have blended and the cheese has dissolved, serve immediately.

Chef's Note: Risotto is the traditional dish served with osso buco. I like making as many dishes ahead of time as possible, but this dish is only good when cooked right before serving.

Artichoke Pie
Preparation time: 20 minutes

1½ cups canned artichoke hearts
2 tablespoons butter
1 small onion, chopped
2 cloves garlic
4 eggs
¼ cup Italian-seasoned bread crumbs
10 ounces Fonseca cheese, shredded
½ teaspoons each fresh oregano and parsley
Salt and pepper

Preheat the oven to 350 degrees. Drain the artichoke hearts and rinse. Chop finely in a food processor, and place into a bowl. Sauté the onion in butter, and add the garlic. Add the artichoke hearts. Beat the eggs, and add to the artichoke mixture. Add the bread crumbs, cheese, oregano, parsley, salt, and pepper. Bake for thirty minutes in a 9" pie plate. Divide into eight pieces and serve.

Chef's Note: It is easy to make this dish ahead of time. Refrigerate, bring to room temperature, and reheat at 325 degrees for fifteen minutes, until the pie is warmed through.

Roasted Asparagus
Preparation time: 15 minutes

4 pounds fresh asparagus
¼ cup olive oil
Sea salt and ground pepper
Juice of half a lemon

Preheat the oven to 325 degrees. Wash the asparagus, and cut off tough ends. Place in a shallow baking dish, and roll the asparagus in the olive oil with salt and pepper. Cook for twenty to twenty-five minutes, depending on the size and age of the asparagus. Do not over-cook. Place a fork in one of the stalks to test for doneness. Squeeze the lemon juice on the asparagus before serving. This will also help to preserve the color.

Chef's Note: Prepare the asparagus with the salt, pepper, and olive oil ahead of your guests' arrival, and follow the cooking directions described above.

Olive-Oil Cake with Orange Sauce
Preparation time: 25 minutes

3 eggs
2 cups granulated sugar
1½ cups good-quality olive oil
1½ cups milk
Grated zest of 3 oranges
½ teaspoon baking soda
½ teaspoon baking powder
2 cups unbleached all-purpose flour
¼ teaspoon nutmeg
¼ teaspoon salt
2 teaspoons confectioner's sugar, for dusting

Preheat the oven to 350 degrees. Butter and flour a twelve-inch spring-form pan. Beat the eggs and sugar together, until the sugar dissolves and the mixture is well blended. Add the olive oil, milk, and orange zest. Continue to mix well. In another bowl, stir together the flour, baking powder, baking soda, nutmeg, and salt. Add these dry ingredients to the egg and olive-oil mixture. Stir until the mixture is well blended. Pour the batter into the prepared pan, and bake for fifty minutes. Test for doneness by inserting a toothpick into the center. If the toothpick comes out clean, the cake is done. If there is some batter on the toothpick, bake for another five minutes. Remove from the oven, and unmold the cake.

Dust the top with the confectioner's sugar, and bring to the table. Pass the orange sauce (see recipe that follows).

Chef's Note: I must confess that this is one of my all-time favorite cakes. It is moist, delicious, and easy to make. Without frosting, it is slightly less caloric.

Orange Sauce
Preparation time: 10 minutes

2 cups strained orange juice
1½ cup sugar
¾ cup port

Combine all three ingredients in a heavy saucepan over medium heat, and bring to a boil. Stir to make sure the sugar dissolves, and then simmer for about thirty minutes, until the sauce has thickened. When ready to serve, pass the sauce in a pretty pitcher or gravy boat for your guests to put a little of the sauce over the cake.

Chef's Note: I like to make this a day or two ahead and refrigerate. On party day, bring to room temperature and warm slightly before serving.

Postmortem
Sam and I, as well as our guests, love opera as much as we do good food. The Puccini opera *Tosca* is a particular favorite of ours. One of our dinner guests is a successful businessman who started his own company. However, his first love is music, and he is blessed with a wonderful voice. He arrived in a good-looking wool jacket with a Japanese-style collar. Bringing forth a CD, he asked if we'd like to hear him sing an aria by the character of Cavaradossi in the last act of *Tosca*, which Puccini wrote in 1900. You can only imagine how delighted we all were.

It is difficult to explain beautiful music with words without sounding hackneyed. In this aria, the hero Cavaradossi is a painter who is put to death because he loves Floria Tosca, the object of Police Chief Baron Scarpia's affection. Just before his execution, Cavaradossi sings "E Lucevan Le Stelle," which, translated into English, means "never was life so dear to me." All of us at our little dinner party within this great universe felt the same as Cavaradossi. Never had life seemed so poignant; it was one of those precious, unexpected moments in life that restores your faith in the beauty of humanity. Our dear friend made Puccini come alive.

He then went on to tell us a marvelous story about the famous conductor of that period, Toscanini. He and Puccini were good friends. Toscanini once fired a bass player after twenty years. On his way out the door, the bass player yelled out to Toscanini, "You are a monster," to which the maestro replied with equal vehemence, "It's too late to apologize."

One of our other guests was a doctor and his wife a former nurse. They brought to light that Puccini had died of throat cancer.

None of us had been to Puccini's villa on Lake Massaciuccoli in the Torre del Lago region, but after this evening we were ready to board the plane. Good music enriches the soul and makes you realize humans are capable of creating great beauty.

First and Last Footnote

As always, I cannot give enough credit to Sam, my wonderful, supportive husband, who is always encouraging, even when the stew is too salty. This book was a journey, and we learned so much along the way. Most of all, we realized that learning is what keeps us young.

When I say we have the best friends in the world, I am not just saying it—it is true. They have patiently participated in all of these theme parties with gusto and excellent suggestions.

In our travels, I have become fascinated by the proverbs of different countries. The Dutch, for example, say, "Normal is crazy enough." The Scots have an amusing proverb: "Forgive your enemy but remember the bastard's name."

One sentence can often describe the essence of a person. Claire Booth Luce once told John Fitzgerald Kennedy that the legacy of a great presidency could be summed up in one sentence. Just for fun, I asked Sam what sentence he felt defined his life. He thought for a moment, got a devilish look on his face, and said, "Forty love, my serve!"

When I die, I hope someone will sum up my life with this simple sentence: "She gave great parties." Hospitality is the linchpin of social interaction. My mother was by far one of the most hospitable people I have ever known. She was a master at making people feel welcome in our home. This hospitality inevitably involved something to eat and drink, even if it was a simple cup of fresh coffee or a hot cup of tea and cookies. My fondest hope is that our children and grandchildren will honor this family tradition. The games of civility and inclusivity are learned, first and foremost, from your family.

Recipes

Miscellaneous

Drinks

List of Images

32982927R00088

Made in the USA
Middletown, DE
25 June 2016